CONNECTING

To order additional copies of *Connecting*, call 1-800-765-6955.
Visit us at www.reviewandherald.com for information
on other Review and Herald products.

CONNECTING

Devotions for Young Adults

TRUDY MORGAN-COLE

REVIEW AND HERALD® PUBLISHING ASSOCIATION
HAGERSTOWN, MD 21740

The author assumes full responsibility for the accuracy of all facts
and quotations as cited in this book.

Texts credited to NIV are from the *Holy Bible, New International Version.*
Copyright © 1973, 1978, 1984, International Bible Society. Used by permission
of Zondervan Bible Publishers.

Texts credited to NKJV are from the New King James Version. Copyright ©
1979, 1980, 1982 by Thomas Nelson, Inc. Used by permission. All rights reserved.

This book was
Edited by Andy Nash
Copyedited by Jocelyn Fay and James Cavil
Cover designed by Saschane Stephenson
Interior design by Mark O'Connor
Electronic makeup by Shirley M. Bolivar
Typeset: 12/14 Bembo

PRINTED IN U.S.A.

06 05 04 03 02   5 4 3 2 1

R&H Cataloging Service
Morgan-Cole, Trudy Jeanne, 1965-
    Connecting: devotions for young adults.

    1. Youth—Prayerbooks and devotions. I. Title

            242.634

ISBN 0-8280-1627-5

This book is dedicated to the young adults
who were youth group members at the
Saint John's Seventh-day Adventist Church
from 1996–2001.
I've never had more fun in my life
than I've had with you guys!

CONTENTS

INTRODUCTION

Intimacy versus isolation. That's what Erik Erikson called it—the conflict people face as they move from their late teens through their 20s and into their early 30s. During those leaving-home, going-to-college, finding-a-job, looking-for-Mr./Ms. Right years we move out of the predictable family relationships that defined us as a child and explore a wide spectrum of new relationships. We have to decide whether to live in isolation or in intimacy with others.

Most of us choose intimacy. At least, we appear to. The true hermits are rare: most of us choose to stay in touch with Mom and Dad and siblings, to hang out with friends, to date and maybe even get married and have kids. We choose to form relationships with others.

But is that real intimacy? Many of us get scared of getting too intimate, even in our closest relationships. We settle for a surface closeness without getting in too deep.

Yet intimacy is where growth happens. Relationships—the good, the bad, and the ugly ones—shape us into who we are. Our most important relationship—our relationship with God—is mostly played out on the game board of our relationships with other people. We learn Christian love, compassion, courage, honesty—all those values—in relationships with others. Being a holy hermit, living in solitary contemplation of the Divine, is easy compared to living in the day-by-day reality of phone calls, broken dates, hurting friends, offended enemies, crying kids, and demanding coworkers.

When we plunge without reservation into the scary world of intimacy with others, we grow spiritually. That's what these stories are about—other people. Relationships. Choosing intimacy. And what we learn from those choices.

Before we get there, a word about how these stories came to be. When I began working on this book, I wanted real-life examples of how young adults had grown through the important relationships in their lives. My own life, rich and fascinating as it has been so far, didn't provide quite enough variety and scope for this, so I e-mailed pretty much every Christian I knew, explaining what my project was and asking for ideas.

I guaranteed people's privacy, even if they didn't ask me to, because I have freely added and changed minor details in these stories. Sometimes I've deliberately changed details to make it difficult to identify someone who really didn't want to be identified. To all of you who helped and contributed: you know who you are. Thanks.

The process was fascinating—discovering the moments and the memories that have been important to such a large group of people. And, of course, I brought a lot of these stories straight out of my own experience. As I write these words, I'm a little on the old side of "young adult" (OK, so I'm 35—I have nothing to hide). By the time you read them, I'll be past that stage of life entirely and onto—h'mmm, what do they call it? Old adult? Middle age? Whatever.

Throughout my own young adult years, intimacy has been a challenge: true intimacy with others, consistent intimacy with God. (I believe the two are closely intertwined.) Which is why I collected these stories and wrote this book. I hope that in reading this, and reflecting on your own relationships and encounters with others, you make some unexpected discoveries.

FRIENDS

In the years we spend traveling away from our "family of origin" and toward our "family of procreation"—in other words, between the time we leave our parents' home and start a family of our own (if we do)—friends are the most important piece of the relationship puzzle. Friends have the power to hold your world together when everything's falling apart. They may not be able to make sense out of everything happening to you, but they're there with you through it.

How many times have you been told that "the friends you make in college [or in academy] will stay with you throughout life"? I was probably told that once a week during my college years. But it's only partly true. Far too many people I once cared deeply about have now become only memories, faces in a yearbook, names signed on treasured cards tucked away in a keepsake box.

But I did make lifelong friends during high school and college and during my first working years. Some are friends I still see, talk to, or e-mail often; others I rarely have contact with, but when we do meet or talk again, it's as though no time has passed, and we're able to pick up right where we left off. I'll always be grateful for those friendships and the way they have helped me grow.

As for the friends I haven't kept in touch with, the ones who seem almost forgotten—I don't believe those relationships are wasted. Life simply doesn't move at a pace that allows us to keep track of everyone we've ever known or cared about, yet every important relationship changes us, shapes who we are. I would not be the person I am today without a college friend I haven't seen or heard from in years. When we meet again someday in heaven, we'll know each other. We'll recognize the imprint we've left on each other's lives.

I think making new friends gets harder as you get older. With rare exceptions, most of us don't make many new close friends once we hit 30. Comedian Jerry Seinfeld has a routine about this, the general idea being that the people you meet after you turn 30 are not any less friendworthy; you like them just as much as the people you met earlier. But all your friend spaces are filled. You're just not taking any new applicants, because you don't need any more friends.

I don't know if that's true for everyone, but it struck a chord with me. And I think it's a shame, because the discovery of friendship is something we should be open to, need to be open to, all through life. I'd like to still be making new friends, and cherishing old ones, when I'm 75. And I'm sure that whatever friends I do have at that point I'll still be learning from.

1.

"YOU SAID HELLO"

Andrea, a new Christian, went off to a Seventh-day Adventist college with lots of hope and a positive outlook. Her naturally cheery, outgoing nature was heightened by her love for the Lord and for everyone around her. She was going to have a great year.

And she did. Andrea liked her classes, loved the social life, made lots of friends, and grew spiritually. From her perspective, life at an Adventist college was everything it was supposed to be.

She met all kinds of people at college—students from around the world, with backgrounds as different from her own as she could possibly imagine. She met lifelong Adventists, rebellious Adventist teenagers, Adventist youth committed to a life of service for the Lord, new converts like herself ablaze with the joy of Jesus.

She also met several non-Adventists, some of whom weren't even Christians. They lived in the surrounding community and came to the college because it was the nearest place to pick up university credits. Laura was like that.

Laura and Andrea sat near each other in Psychology of the Exceptional Child. They smiled at each other and said hello at the beginning of each class. A couple times they worked in a group together. Andrea rarely saw Laura outside of class, since Laura lived off campus and came to the college only when she had a class. They didn't become close friends, but they were friendly.

The year drew to a close, and Andrea got busy packing up her dorm room, preparing for her summer job. She studied for exams and attended her last few classes. On the last day of Psychology of the Exceptional Child Laura said, "Well, I guess I'll see you around. Although maybe not—I'm finished with my classes here, so I won't be around next year. Good luck anyway." As she turned to go, she slipped an envelope into Andrea's hand.

Andrea put the envelope in her notebook and said goodbye to the teacher and a few other friends from class. She didn't remember Laura's envelope until she was on her way to lunch. When she sat down at her table in the cafeteria, she finally opened it and found a card inside.

Wow, how nice of her to give me a card, Andrea thought. *It's not as if we were close friends.*

The outside of the card showed a pretty nature scene and the words "Thank You." Inside was a message in Laura's own handwriting.

Dear Andrea,

As this school year draws to a close I just wanted to say thank you for being a friend. Your cheerful "Hello" at the beginning of class each day was the high point of my day on campus. I always appreciated your optimism, enthusiasm, and warmth.

I didn't get to know many people well this year, I guess because I didn't live on campus and wasn't around for any extracurricular activities.

I really never felt like I fit in with the clique around here. Coming to a Christian college, I guess I just assumed that everyone would be friendly and outgoing. But most days yours was the only "Hello" I got.

Again, thanks so much for making this year better for me.

Laura

Andrea stared at the card in her hand. Most days yours was the only *"Hello" I got. . . . Coming to a Christian college, I just assumed . . .*

Her "friendship" with Laura had been one of the least significant things in Andrea's school year. It had cost her no time, no effort, barely any thought to say "Hi" to Laura and make a little small talk when they met in class. But for Laura it had been the high point of her campus experience.

Andrea looked around at the laughing, talking students all

around her. *It shouldn't have been that way!* she wanted to stand on a table and yell. *We should have done more! I should have done more! Is this the best we can do for a non-Christian right in the middle of our campus?*

It's been said so often that it's become trite—a trite-but-true formula: Christian schools don't necessarily equal a Christlike, welcoming atmosphere. Far too many people, both inside the church fold and out of it, have found cliquishness, coolness, even outright rejection and cruelty to be the norm rather than the exception on a Christian campus.

And yes, maybe they were the people who didn't try hard enough themselves to be outgoing and friendly, who had a chip on their shoulder, who didn't fit in for one reason or another. Those are the excuses, the defenses, we make. Written down here on paper, they look as lame as they are.

It shouldn't be that way. Andrea knew it, you know it, I know it. Even Laura knew it. She knew that the Christian gospel promised something different from what she actually found when she went to study among Christian people.

I could end this here—just trying to make you feel guilty. Or I could try to come up with a solution—when we all know there isn't one, short of the Spirit of Christ totally taking over the heart of every Christian student on campus. That's what we pray for and hope for, yet in our own lives we still resist.

So that's where I'm going to end—in our own lives. Be Andrea in this story. Make her choice—to say that hello, to start that conversation. Take it a step further. Make time in your life for someone who doesn't fit there neatly.

I can turn this back on myself just as easily. Andrea is a friend of mine, and I'm about 1 percent as friendly and outgoing as she is. When she told me this story I thought, *I would have been one of the people ignoring Laura.* Not because I wouldn't have liked her—just because I wouldn't have made the effort.

I want to make the effort. It takes so little—as Andrea discovered—to make a lasting impact on someone. To make an eternal impact would take a little more. But it would be worth it, wouldn't it?

CONNECTING

**A word fitly spoken is like apples
of gold in settings of silver.
Proverbs 25:11, NKJV.**

THINK IT THROUGH

1. Think of a time when someone has "fitly spoken" the word you needed to hear at a particular time. Have you done the same for someone else?

2. Do you wish you were more friendly, able to reach out better to others? If so, what keeps you from doing so?

2.

FOLDED LAUNDRY

Marie and I haven't talked in a while. Neither of us can believe that it's possible to get months behind on answering a friend's e-mail—I mean, how much easier could it get to stay in touch? Once in a while we phone. I send a Christmas card and letter. When we do talk, it doesn't take long before the gap of time and distance is erased and we're talking and laughing together as we did when we saw each other every day. Old friends are great that way.

We shared a lot together once . . . high points and low points in both our lives. When Marie's baby was born her mother phoned me at 2:00 a.m. to let me know. And I didn't mind being woken up—I would have been offended if she *hadn't* called. That's how close we were.

We shared our faith then too. Marie hadn't grown up a Seventh-day Adventist, or even a Christian, but when we met she had recently met Jesus and been baptized. She was alive with her faith. Talking about God, praying for each other—that was part of who we were as friends.

Time passed. Life happened. We moved in different directions, geographically speaking. Our lives moved in similar directions, though—we both got married, had two children. I was a bridesmaid at her wedding. She was supposed to fly down to be a bridesmaid at mine, but her second baby was born just before and she wasn't quite up to it. We were still close enough then that her absence was a gap in my celebration.

But in the years since, as I said, we've slipped behind on keeping in touch. And despite our similar lifestyles, we're aware of differences, too. I've stayed active in my church; my faith is still the central thing in my life. Marie no longer goes to church. Her husband's not a Christian, and she's drifted away. I haven't asked how far away, or how she feels about God now. We haven't discussed that.

Until the last time we talked. Because she's on my e-mail list, she'd gotten my "Help! I'm writing a devotional book!" message, in which I asked a lot of friends to share important moments in their lives and relationships—ideas that were to help get me started on this book.

When Marie called, she said, "Your e-mail sent me into kind of a tailspin." She began to talk about how she missed having God in her life, having a spiritual center. We talked about that certainty and peace you have when you're close to the Lord—that feeling you don't get from anything else in life, not even your husband or kids, precious as they are. How she misses having that feeling and wants it back.

She said, "I started thinking about when I was at academy—the things that made me want to become a Christian." Her divorced parents had sent her to an Adventist academy when she was 14—just because they wanted her in a good-quality boarding school, somewhere safe but away from home. She knew nothing about Seventh-day Adventists when she landed on campus.

"It was the little things that made a difference to me," Marie went on. "Like how friendly everyone was . . . and how nice the teachers were. One Christmas my family told me it wouldn't work out for me to come home, so I had to spend Christmas at school. The teachers who were there were so nice, so welcoming to me— inviting me over, things like that. The boys' dean gave me a Christmas present. I couldn't imagine any of the public school teachers I knew doing anything like that."

In the girls' dorm, though, there were the usual adolescent arguments, the obligatory rebels; there was also a warmth Marie hadn't found anywhere else. "I would go into the laundry room to take my stuff out of the dryer, and someone would have taken it out already, and have it all folded for me. That amazed me—that a total stranger would do that. You know—random acts of kindness."

Folded laundry. Random acts of kindness. The little things we do—or don't do—that can matter so little or so much. For Marie, looking back over the gap of 15 years, those little things stand out as signposts on her path to meeting Jesus.

In my dormitory days I often took someone else's laundry out of the dryer when it was time to put mine in. I think I usually left it in a pile on top of the dryer. I'm not that big into folding laundry, even my own. I don't think anyone's going to be kept out of heaven because I didn't fold their laundry. But it gives me pause for thought.

More than I wonder about laundry, I wonder about Marie. Whether her need to make God the center of her life again will be strong enough to pull her back to Him, back to church, back to commitment. I wonder what signposts, what random acts of kindness, might lead her along that road again. I wish I lived close enough to fold her laundry, or meet her for lunch, or whatever would help.

I pray, of course. In fact, a couple years ago I put Marie and her family at the top of my prayer list, making time every day for special prayer that she would come back to church and bring her husband and kids with her. For a while I prayed earnestly, fervently. I didn't see any results, so gradually I forgot about praying. God doesn't forget. God's awareness of people is not, fortunately, depending on my remembering to pray for them. His Spirit keeps working, searching for an opening, long after my attention has wandered.

Now Marie's on the top of my prayer list again. After we spoke the other day, I e-mailed her. By the time you read this, a lot more time will have passed. I hope that Marie will be where she wants to be spiritually, that we can again share that faith we shared when we were first friends. But I don't know. I hope there's some Christian near her who believes in random acts of kindness.

CONNECTING

**If anyone gives even a cup of cold water
to one of these little ones because he is my
disciple, I tell you the truth, he will certainly not
lose his reward. Matthew 10:42, NIV.**

THINK IT THROUGH

1. Do you really believe your most casual acts could influence someone's eternal choices? If so, how does that make you feel?

2. Do you ever do "random acts of kindness"? Have you ever been the recipient of one? Can you think of one you could do today?

3. If it's true that God's Spirit keeps working on people even when we neglect to pray for them, why does He want us to pray?

3.

"SOMEONE NEEDED ME"

It seemed impossible. They were a healthy couple in their late 20s. The last life crisis Jenni ever expected to be facing was her husband's cancer diagnosis.

But it had happened. The good news was that the doctors were optimistic. They felt the surgery would give Tim an excellent chance of survival. Timing was crucial, so with only a few days' notice Jenni and Tim prepared for his surgery.

Jenni was frightened. She felt suddenly alone in the world. Her own family lived far away, and until now she and Tim had felt completely self-sufficient, just the two of them. Now Jenni needed someone to share her fear with. She needed to be strong for Tim, but she had to have someone to lean on.

Specifically, she needed someone to go to the hospital with her, to sit beside her during those endless hours in the waiting room during his surgery, to be there for her when she saw him after surgery, while she waited for him to speak to her again, while she waited to hear—what? News that would change her life. She needed a hand to hold, a shoulder to cry on, a friend who would know how to sit quietly and simply be there.

Fortunately, she had a friend like that. Jenni's best friend, Anne, quickly agreed. "I would love to come to the hospital with you," she said. "I'd be so happy to know there was something I could do to help you through all this."

CONNECTING

The night before the surgery Jenni and Tim were busy packing, organizing, trying not to say the things that would make them both cry. The phone rang several times that night—faraway family, nearby friends, all wanting to offer prayers and love and support. Then the phone rang again. It was Anne.

"Jenni, I'm so sorry, I'm so sorry," she croaked into the phone. Jenni could hardly hear her best friend's voice. "I've come down with this flu bug—I can hardly get out of bed."

Jenni's heart sank. "That's all right, don't worry—"

"No, it's not me I'm worried about. You know I'd come be with you no matter how lousy I was feeling . . ." Anne stopped to blow her nose. ". . . but I don't think I should go to the hospital with the flu like this. I shouldn't be around sick people—especially Tim."

"Oh, you're right, of course you're right," Jenni said. "No, you'd better stay home."

"Will you be able to get someone else to go with you?"

"Of course I will. Don't worry about it. Just take care and get well."

"OK. Phone me when the surgery's over. Let me know how it went?"

After Anne hung up, Jenni stared at the phone, mentally running through her list of close friends. She knew Sheila was out of town. Denise wouldn't be able to take time off work at such short notice. She phoned Rachel, who was really sorry but said she had a big meeting at work the next day that she couldn't possibly get out of.

Jenni was faced with the possibility that she might have to go to the hospital—sit through her husband's life-or-death surgery—entirely alone. She couldn't stand the thought. She was relying on God for strength, but she needed another human hand to hold, a face she could see, a voice she could hear. That was when she thought of Diane.

Jenni didn't know Diane as well as her other friends. They had met only a short while ago at church, since Diane was new in the area. They were about the same age and shared some common interests, and in the couple conversations they'd had over potluck casseroles in the church dining hall they'd hit it off well. But Jenni didn't feel she knew Diane well enough to ask something like this. They hadn't even visited in each other's homes yet.

But she was getting desperate. She didn't want to go alone. So she picked up the phone and called Diane.

When she explained the situation, Diane—who already knew about Tim's surgery—said, "Oh, Jenni, I'd be so happy to go with you. Thank you so much for asking me!"

"Really, Diane? That's great. We're leaving really early tomorrow—oh, but you'd better take your own car; there's no back seat in ours."

"Um, I don't have a car."

"Oh, no. The only place to ride in ours is in the hatchback—and you can't ride in there for two and a half hours."

"Yes, I can. I'll do it."

So the next morning, in the gray of early dawn, Jenni and Tim drove by Diane's apartment building. She twisted her body into the shape of a pretzel and climbed into the hatchback of their Honda, and they made the long drive to the hospital.

Diane stayed with Jenni through the whole ordeal. She was there to talk with Jenni and keep the hours from dragging too slowly while Tim was in surgery. She was there when the doctor told Jenni that the surgery looked as though it had been a complete success. She waited just outside the room while Jenni went in to see Tim—who looked like a helpless stranger, trapped in a maze of tubes and monitors. Diane was there to hug Jenni and let her cry when she came out.

When night came, Jenni asked Diane if there was anyone she could call for a ride back home. Jenni planned to stay at the hospital all night. "I could call my brother," she said, "but I'll stay here with you tonight."

Tim recovered in the hospital for five days after his surgery. Jenni stayed the whole time—and so did Diane. Diane went home a couple nights, but always returned the next day. She was there to share with Jenni the joy of seeing Tim get better and stronger. In the long afternoons and the late nights, while Tim slept, Jenni and Diane talked. Over those five days Jenni and Diane went from being casual acquaintances to being close friends.

CONNECTING

Diane was also there for Jenni during the long weeks and months of Tim's convalescence at home. Family and other friends were around too, but Diane remained a consistent support, dropping by with casseroles, sending encouraging notes, calling to see how things were going.

It's been five years since Tim's surgery. He's in great health; his cancer hasn't returned. For Jenni and Tim, life has pretty much returned to normal.

Jenni still considers Diane one of her best friends. One day, over lunch, they discussed the depression that Diane had struggled with for many years. "When we first got to know each other—when I first moved here—that was one of my really low times," Diane said.

Jenni nodded. She knew that Diane had moved to the area after breaking up with her college boyfriend, and that she'd endured a long period of depression as a result.

"What I never told you," Diane said, "is how bad it was. Right around the time I met you—in fact, right before you called to ask me to come to the hospital with you—I was thinking about suicide."

"Oh, no—really?" Jenni asked.

"Yeah. I don't know if I really would have done it, but I'd gone pretty far in planning it—lined up some pills and everything. Just a day or so before we went to the hospital I was right on the brink of doing it. Something stopped me—God, I guess. But I just had this feeling, like I was of no value, like I didn't matter to anyone in this world."

Jenni had no words. She lightly covered Diane's hand with her own.

"When you called me, I felt so honored that you had thought of me—I knew it was because Anne wasn't able to go, but still, I just thought, *Wow!* We didn't even know each other that well, but you thought of me. You needed me. All those days in the hospital—it was the first time in a long time I felt like someone needed me, like I had some value to someone."

Diane looked up from her plate and smiled. "You thought you needed someone to go to the hospital with you and Tim—but you could never have known how much *I* needed *you.*"

"Someone Needed Me"

A friend loves at all times, and a brother is born for adversity. Proverbs 17:17, NIV.

THINK IT THROUGH

1. Have you ever resisted asking a friend for help because you were afraid to impose upon them or thought they might say no? Could Jenni and Diane's story make a difference in your outlook?

2. If you feel the way Diane did—as though no one needs or values you—and a friend like Jenni *doesn't* call to ask for your help, what could you do to assure yourself that you are of value?

3. Is there a "Diane" in your life today? Can you let someone know that you need them?

4.

"*SUCH* A NICE GUY!"

Somebody once said (I think it was in a movie) that the cruelest words a woman can say to a man are "You're such a nice guy." Mainly because that sentence is generally followed by the word "but"—as in ". . . but I couldn't see myself dating you" or ". . . but you're just not my type." You get the idea.

I've described several guys as "nice" in my time, including the one I eventually married, so it can't be too derogatory. But thanks to one particular guy, the phrase still has the ability to send cold shivers down my back . . . and to make me meditate on such subjects as gossip, guilt, and friendship.

Aaron really *was* a nice guy. He was quiet, thoughtful, and kind. I had a crush on his roommate in college, so I hung out with Aaron a fair bit. In the end I dated the roommate for a blindingly brief period, but he became a good friend—and so did Aaron.

Summertime came, and I moved out of the dorm and into an off-campus apartment with my cousin. Actually, it wasn't exactly an apartment. My cousin was renting one of a row of little mini-town-houses just on the fringe of campus—very low-budget student housing (is there any other kind?). But these little dwellings, although as tiny as your average apartment, were indeed little individual row houses, each with a back door, front door, even a tiny basement.

One evening Aaron dropped by to visit me and my cousin. He stayed a couple hours, hanging out in the living room, talking, lis-

26

tening to music. The conversation wasn't very exciting. Most of the things Aaron liked to talk about—his classes, his car, some kind of electronic project he was working on in his dorm room—weren't particularly interesting to me. I liked having him around; he was nice and friendly, but I didn't exactly hang on his every word when he was talking.

I guess this particular evening had just gone on a little long. When Aaron finally got up to go, I walked out with him to the back door, which was located at the bottom of the basement stairs, and said good night. Then I walked up the stairs to the kitchen where my cousin was washing the dishes.

"Aaron is *such* a nice guy," she said.

"Yes . . . and *so* boring!" I said, laughing.

My cousin didn't laugh. She was looking over my shoulder with a frozen-horror expression. She pointed. I looked behind me. The window over my shoulder was wide open.

I didn't dare look outside to see if Aaron was still in hearing range. I just froze, wishing I could call those words back. I liked Aaron. He was a nice guy. He was my friend. Yes, I thought he was boring sometimes, but I didn't want *him* to know I thought that.

I lived in an agony of guilt for the rest of the night and the following day. At one point I actually timed how long it took me to walk up the stairs, enter the kitchen, and reply to the phrase "He's such a nice guy." Then I went out the back door and walked at what I thought might be Aaron's pace for that same period of time—I think it was 17 seconds—to see how far away from the house I was. Then I got my cousin to say something in the kitchen, with the window still open, to see if I could possibly hear her. I couldn't. But I still wasn't sure Aaron hadn't heard me. After all, anyone who's ever talked to me can tell you I have a very carrying voice.

I thought of calling him to say, "I don't know if you heard me say anything after you left last night, but if you did, I'm really sorry, and if you didn't, please forget we ever had this conversation." But somehow I didn't think this would make matters better. I prayed earnestly, "God, please let him not have heard it," although I didn't see how even God could change what had already happened.

CONNECTING

Perhaps He could strike Aaron with a very selective form of amnesia, with which he would forget only the first five minutes after leaving my house that evening.

Then there was the long drawn-out horror of waiting till I ran into Aaron again, waiting to see if he acted any differently toward me. Surely that would tell me whether he'd heard me or not. But of course it didn't. He was such a quiet guy anyway that it was impossible to tell if he was secretly hurt or offended. I would manage to convince myself that he was acting perfectly normal and couldn't have heard my comment, and then we'd meet on campus and I'd spend a half hour dissecting the tone of his "Hello," to see if it meant he was offended.

I will freely admit that in my life, both before that incident and after, I have made hundreds—no, thousands—of casually insulting comments about people I considered good friends. I talk behind people's backs. Admit it—you do it too. Virtually everyone who talks at all has criticized people behind their back—even people we like.

This time was different. This time there was a good possibility my friend might have heard me.

Obviously, I'd be having some very different conversations if I thought my family, friends, and enemies could overhear everything I said. And perhaps it would do me a world of good to pretend that they could. It certainly would make me more cautious about those cutting, casual criticisms. And my ardent desire to turn back time just those few moments, just so I could have never made that comment, illustrated vividly how impossible it is to take back words once they're spoken.

But what really got me about this incident was the towering load of guilt I felt. Not because it was such a heinous sin—up against murder and grand larceny, calling someone "boring" seems like pretty small stuff. What got me about this particular sin was that I realized, with total clarity, how much potential it had to hurt someone I cared about.

I wish (sometimes, when I'm at my best) that I had the ability to see all sin in that clear, unflattering light. If I could see how every unkind word, every thoughtless act, every casual cruelty, could hurt someone else. If I could see how each of these sins has the power to break the heart of one of God's precious children. If I could see how every sin hurts God Himself—then, surely then, I would think before I speak, pause before I act, and let the Spirit take over instead.

I wish I could. I hope I would. But still, despite that revelation, I go on criticizing and cracking jokes at other people's expense. I'm half afraid I'll never learn until someone *really* overhears me. I'm almost afraid to think whom I might have to hurt before I really believe in the power of the tongue that the apostle James wrote about so eloquently.

By the way, I never did find out if Aaron heard me that night. I left campus shortly after, and in the following school year we moved into different circles of friends and didn't see each other as much. I've seen him only once in all the years since college, when we ran into each other by accident and he took me out for a very nice dinner. Which is what you'd expect him to do—because he was, and still is, a truly nice guy.

> **The tongue is a small part of the body, but it makes great boasts. Consider what a great forest is set on fire by a small spark. The tongue also is a fire, a world of evil among the parts of the body. It corrupts the whole person, sets the whole course of his life on fire, and is itself set on fire by hell. All kinds of animals, birds, reptiles and creatures of the sea are being tamed and have been tamed by man, but no man can tame the tongue. It is a restless evil, full of deadly poison. With the tongue we praise our Lord and Father, and with it we curse men, who have been made in God's likeness. Out of the same mouth come praise and cursing. My brothers, this should not be. James 3:5-10, NIV.**

CONNECTING

1. Is it ever possible to tame the power of the tongue? If so, how?

2. What would you have done or said differently yesterday and today, if your words and actions were being seen and heard by everyone you knew?

3. Is it ever acceptable to talk about people behind their backs? Should we adopt a zero-tolerance policy on gossip and criticism of all kinds? Is that even possible?

5.

A $100 BILL

Todd and Karen had been married only a couple years. They had a toddler and a new baby on the way, and Todd was in medical school. He worked part-time along with his heavy class load, and Karen taught piano and voice lessons. They had taken out a loan to buy a small house in a rundown neighborhood, and they worked long hours after work and school fixing up the basement so they could rent out the apartment to other students.

They scraped by financially, but only just. The new baby turned out to be twins. Food for the children was top priority, but their budget was bare minimum. They had no luxuries, and sometimes Todd took peanut-butter sandwiches to lunch every day for a week.

The little church they attended was friendly and welcoming, and they soon became active members there. Church members knew the young couple were struggling to make ends meet, and they helped as much as they could.

One week their vacuum cleaner died. If you've never had three tiny children, you may not appreciate how difficult it is to survive in a houseful of crawlers and toddlers without a vacuum cleaner. To Todd and Karen, the loss of the vacuum was a major disaster, but they simply had no spare money to replace it.

Except $100 they had set aside for that month's tithe. They were seriously tempted. They went as far as to pick up the sealed tithe envelope and turn it over in their hands, wondering if God would understand. But in the end they agreed: they'd made a commitment to put God first in everything, and that meant in their finances, too.

That Sabbath Todd, Karen, little Kayla, and the twin boys came to church as usual. Nothing in their appearance or their cheery attitude hinted that they were in need. They were trying hard to trust that God would work everything out.

Karen took the children to cradle roll and sat through "Jesus loves the little ones like me, me, me," trying hard to put her faith in God's love and concern. Todd taught the juniors and earliteens about God, who sees the fall of every sparrow. In church they sat together and sang, "Oh yes, He cares—I know He cares."

After church they chatted and shook hands with friends on the porch. The pastor came up to Todd with an envelope in his hand. "This isn't from me," he said. "I'm not allowed to tell you who gave it to me, but someone very much wanted you to have this."

Todd and Karen exchanged a quick glance; Todd said thank you to the pastor and pocketed the envelope. Out in the car after church they opened it—no note, nothing but a $100 bill. God's answer to their immediate need; a touch from an anonymous friend.

Years later the incident still shines in Todd's and Karen's minds. Their little family is quite secure now, long removed from the days when bills were scary, grocery shopping was a challenge, and a broken vacuum cleaner was a major disaster. Todd and Karen don't know the name of the friend who cared enough to give $100. It could have been one of several people. But they remember that someone reached out in answer to their unspoken need.

When Todd told me this story his focus was on God's providence—they had chosen to return their tithe faithfully, and God had provided, as He's promised to do. That's a powerful lesson, but my attention was drawn to the human agent God acted through—the nameless friend who didn't know about the broken vacuum cleaner, but simply responded to Spirit's call and put $100 in an envelope with no idea how much it was needed.

In contrast, I thought of two other stories. One was of my college friend Mitch, who was extremely short of cash. He had no financial support from his family and was barely able to afford food, much less pay his escalating school bills. He also was a remarkably poor financial manager and had absolutely no ability to set priorities. One day an envelope appeared in his mailbox. As with Todd's envelope, this donation ($25) was anonymous, but it did contain a handwritten note: "My God will meet all your needs according to his glorious riches in Christ Jesus" (Philippians 4:19, NIV).

Mitch was grateful. At the time he was living on bread and butter, since he couldn't afford to eat in the cafeteria. But he spent the $25 on two cassette tapes of his favorite band.

I narrowly avoided strangling Mitch. Mostly I just felt sorry for the person who had cared enough to give him cash, and hoped they never found out what he did with the money. I assume it's the fear of putting our hard-earned cash in the hands of a Mitch that keeps most of us from making more of these generous gestures.

I also thought of Trish. Trish was a single mom with a small baby, and a good friend of mine. She lived in the same town as Todd and Karen did, during those same years when Todd was in medical school. She attended the same little church. And she struggled with the same bills, the same fears and frustrations.

Unlike Todd and Karen, Trish didn't attend church regularly. She found it hard—living on her own with a baby, no husband, and no car—to get out to church. Her baby wasn't old enough to get much out of Sabbath school, and she couldn't sit through an entire church service with him, so sometimes it seemed pointless. She was new in town, and as a single woman with a baby she felt embarrassed meeting church members—after all, the only thing they knew about her was that she'd had sex before she was married.

So Trish went to church once every couple months, usually when I came down to visit her. On her fifth or sixth visit, the pastor, to whom she'd been introduced twice, shook her hand and said how nice it was to have a visitor—where was she from? She was sad that he hadn't even recognized her. "But it's my fault," she said. "I should go to church more often."

That friendly, warm little church threw no showers for Trish and her baby. Nobody left bags of groceries outside her door or slipped her a $100 bill in the foyer. Which makes me wonder—what does it take to elicit a warm, generous response from us Christians? Do you have to prove you're deserving and pretty much sinless? Or do you have to jump up and down in front of us and say "I'm here! I'm in need!" to make sure you don't get overlooked?

I don't tell these stories about Mitch and Trish to diminish in any way the wonderful experience that Todd and Karen had. Theirs was an example of a time when things worked the way they're supposed to work all the time with God's people, God's church—when God used friends to touch each other's lives with blessing. I just wish it had worked out better for Mitch, better for Trish. Mostly, though, I wish I could do a better job of keeping my eyes open, of listening when God the Spirit points out to me the person who could use an unsigned gift.

> **My God will meet all your needs according
> to his glorious riches in Christ Jesus.
> Philippians 4:19, NIV.**

THINK IT THROUGH

1. Do you find it easier to give an anonymous gift or to identify yourself as the giver? Why?

2. Have you ever had the urge to be generous to someone and failed to respond? What held you back?

3. How much do you think God really cares whether we're faithful with tithe paying? Do we make too big a deal of that?

6.

"I DON'T KNOW WHAT TO SAY"

The youth social is ending; friends and visitors drift away from the academy gym. The youth leadership team and a few other volunteers are left to help my husband and me with the cleanup. Together we wash glasses, pick up garbage, sweep the floors, take down decorations, and replace tables and desks. We break down the sound system last so the speakers can keep blaring contemporary Christian music while we work.

Rebecca, usually one of the hardest workers on the team, isn't helping tonight. She's out in the porch talking to Kevin. Almost every youth social we have wraps up with one of the girls having a one-on-one, heart-to-heart with Kevin in the hallway or in the porch or out on the steps. Sometimes they rotate so that at least one girl is tied up all evening long, listening to Kevin.

It's a scene so familiar to me I could write the script, even though I never eavesdrop on the conversations. The visuals tell me all I need to know: Kevin slumped against a wall or kicking the ground angrily; Rebecca (or Suzanne or Emily) sitting or standing beside him, leaning forward earnestly, eyes bright, sure she's going to find just the right words to break through his anger and sadness.

Kevin isn't even part of the youth group—his family doesn't belong to our church, and he never goes to our worship activities, because he's angry at God. But he goes to all the social activities because he's friends with our whole group. And one after another, kids in the youth group—mostly the girls, but the guys, too—bring up his name in prayer requests and tell me that we need to find some way to help Kevin, because he's so depressed, he's so angry, he's so rebellious, he's so . . .

I like Kevin, and I wish I could find a way to help him. But I can't help feeling, as I said, how familiar this all is. I could time-travel back half a lifetime to my own teenage years, clip Kevin out of the picture and replace him with Derek, and the scene would be exactly the same.

Derek was angry, often depressed, and rebellious. He was fascinated with God and religion, yet bitter against God. I and a half dozen other Christian girls gave our best shot at saving him (it didn't hurt that he was fairly gorgeous). At one point he did accept the Lord, but he drifted away again.

Then there was Neil. He went to our church and had been one of the "good kids"—in our day he and I were on the youth leadership team; we were the ones who stayed behind to clean up after the socials. We planned Sabbath school and vespers programs together. Then, when he was 16, Neil decided to rebel. He started to drink and party. I remember him sitting in my car (well, my mother's car—I was only 17 and had just gotten my license) flicking cigarette ash out the windows while I cried and pleaded with him to change his ways. I answered emergency calls to come pick him up at parties when he was drunk, and listened to him rage about how meaningless life was. When I went away to college I didn't know how Neil would manage without me.

In college there was Jordan, who thought he might be gay and was struggling with the conflict between his sexual orientation and his Christian standards. And there was Rick, whom I actually dated for most of a year, who was so constantly in need of encouragement and cheering up that, looking back, I realize he must have been clinically depressed and in need of professional help.

But somehow, with all these guys and a half dozen more, I still believed that my hours of listening, talking, encouraging, reasoning, shouting, crying, and writing would make a difference.

My superhero complex ended abruptly with my first teaching job. I was barely 21, teaching high school, and almost immediately I'd collected a heartful of strays who needed love, attention, motivation, and help of all kinds. (Again, mostly guys. I really think this urge to save another person happens most often across gender lines—maybe there's a kind of attraction that accompanies it.)

Of the students whose needs almost overwhelmed me that first year, the one I was drawn to most was Andrew, whose sense of humor and view of life were so like my own. He was a funny, sensitive high school senior who was also hurting far more than I realized. I thought I was helping him—till he attempted suicide.

Fortunately, it wasn't a very successful attempt, and Andrew was soon back at school, where I plunged wholeheartedly into my usual routine of trying to solve his problems and break through his loneliness and alienation. Nothing helped. Then one day I lent him a book—not because I thought it was a book that would help him particularly, but just because it was one I liked and thought he might enjoy reading.

Well, Andrew came to the Lord because of that book, and years later, still a Christian, he gives me credit for helping him find God—not because of any of the careful and concerned things I said to him, but because I so offhandedly lent him the very book that happened to speak to him. Accidentally, I did the right thing. Or rather, I happened to be standing by when the Spirit did the right thing.

I don't know if it was Andrew's experience, or the realization that as a teacher I could drown emotionally if I let myself get so wrapped up in every needy student, but that year marked a change for me. I stepped back. I put a little distance between myself and other people's problems. I finally, slowly, began to realize that God is in the business of saving people. I am not.

Now I'm twice Rebecca's age, watching her wring her warm, generous heart dry over Kevin, and there are things I want to tell her. So I try. Late in the evening, when another girl has taken over listening to Kevin, Rebecca comes in to help clean up, and together we sweep the floor, me holding the dustpan while she pushes dirt ahead of the broom.

"What can you say to someone who's so depressed?" she asks me. "I feel so helpless, as though nothing I can say will help him." We're yelling to be heard because the music is turned up so loud, but the wall of sound around us makes our conversation seem as intimate as a whisper.

I take a deep breath, consider dodging the issue, and decide to tell her the truth. "There really *is* nothing you can say, Rebecca," I tell her. "You feel helpless because you are helpless. You can be there for your friends and listen to them, but you can't solve their problems. Only God can do that."

She doesn't like this answer, of course, and she keeps trying, in different words, to find the answer *she* needs. "But . . . how can I help him? What can I say? I don't know what to say to him."

"Listen to him, Rebecca, and pray for him. I wish I'd spent half the time praying for my friends that I spent talking and worrying. But don't let his problems drag you down. You can't solve them— only God can."

I'm repeating myself. It's time to stop talking. If someone had told me these things when I was 16, would I have heard them? Probably not.

Letting go when you love people is scary. Recognizing that God is in control and you aren't is scary. Realizing that even God has surrendered some measure of His divine control to allow for human free will is scariest of all—because it means that someone we love *might* choose, ultimately, not to follow Him. And we can't fix that.

But we can know that the Spirit will do everything within the tremendous resources of divinity—anything short of sheer force—to win that one person's heart. We can know that God loves our friend a million times more than we ever could. We can love and pray and listen. But we can't fix it, and we aren't called to crush ourselves under the weight of someone else's burden.

I look back over the thumbnail sketches of friends I wrote about in these paragraphs. Some, like Andrew and Neil, are walking with the Lord and still growing in Him. Some, like Derek, still seem distant from Him. Others, like Rick and Jordan, I've lost touch with. One thing's for sure: whatever has happened to them, I didn't do it. If I was faithful to God, if I said the right thing or lent the right book at the right moment, then He was able to use me, and I'll praise Him for that.

I've written in the pages before these about a friend whose casual "Hello" made a difference in someone's life, about another friend who was drawn to Christianity by acts as simple as a fellow student folding her laundry. Of course, the things we do count—sometimes more than we know. But if we had to plot and plan exactly what words, what acts, would change another person's life, we'd go insane. We agonize and worry over our friends and our influence on them just as if we were in control of the whole grand design. Peace and freedom comes with the realization that we're not.

Someday we'll all know the result of every prayer we prayed, every word we spoke, every act we performed. But in that day too we'll know that the burden didn't rest on our shoulders. It never should have. He held our loved ones in His hands all along.

I hope Rebecca figures that out sooner than I did.

God is faithful, by whom you were called into the fellowship of His Son, Jesus Christ our Lord. 1 Corinthians 1:9, NKJV.

I know whom I have believed, and am convinced that he is able to guard what I have entrusted to him for that day. 2 Timothy 1:12, NIV.

THINK IT THROUGH

1. Why is it so difficult to trust God with the lives of people we care about?

2. To what extent is God totally "in control" of everything that happens? Can human free will sabotage God's will?

3. Other than prayer, what do you think is the most effective thing you can do for a hurting or rebellious friend?

7.

"THINGS CAN'T GET ANY WORSE"

A few years ago my friend Jessica had a very bad summer. It started when her apartment was broken into one afternoon. Thieves stole several valuables and trashed the place. Like lots of people who rent apartments, Jessica had no insurance on her belongings, so she lost her TV, stereo, computer, and a number of smaller items.

She couldn't handle going back to the apartment right away—besides the mess, it was just so scary. She felt vulnerable. So she packed a lot of stuff in her car that night and drove to a friend's house several miles away. On the way her car broke down. She got it towed to the garage, and her friend came to pick her up. The next day Jessica got the bad news: her transmission was shot. She didn't have several hundred dollars to spend on a repair job right then, so she was effectively homeless and carless.

A couple weeks later, as Jessica worked on getting her apartment straightened out, getting the courage to sleep there again, and getting someone to fix her car cheaply, she heard from her parents. Her mom had been in the hospital for a series of tests, and the results weren't good. It looked as though she had cancer.

Jessica was devastated. Her parents sent money for her to fly home for her mom's surgery, so she put her house and car problems on the back burner and got ready to travel home. We went out for lunch the day before she left. "I just can't believe all the stuff that's happened lately," she said, running both hands through her hair. She looked exhausted. "Just keep on praying for me, OK?"

"You know I will," I promised.

I went on my own vacation while Jessica was away. I bought a postcard to send her, and on the back I wrote, "Hope your mom's doing OK. I'm still praying for you. Keep your courage up—at least you know things can't get any worse!"

When Jessica and I both got back from our trips, she called and said she needed to see me. We went for a long walk together down our favorite riverside trail. "You know when you wrote me that card, saying things couldn't get any worse?" she asked, her voice caught between laughter and tears. "Well, they did."

"Oh no. What happened?" I already knew her mother's surgery had gone well, so I couldn't imagine what else could have happened.

It took a while for the story to come out, because Jessica hadn't yet shared it with anyone. But it turned out that while she was home she had gone out for the evening with an ex-boyfriend who got pushy and aggressive later in the evening. Jessica had never slept with this guy—in fact, she was still a virgin, waiting for the right guy and marriage to come along. But her old boyfriend wouldn't take no for an answer. Jessica was date-raped in the living room of her parents' empty house.

I was horrified. And I was so sorry for penning those light-hearted, thoughtless words. Apparently, in this sinful world, things can always get worse.

As we walked past the river lazily unwinding in late-summer sunlight, Jessica poured out her pain and hurt. Finally I asked, "Jessica, are you mad at God?"

The question seemed to take her by surprise, though if I'd been in her situation it would have been right at the front of my mind. "Mad at God? No; why should I be?"

"Well, so much bad stuff has happened, and you're a good Christian—maybe He should be protecting you. Don't you blame Him for letting these things happen to you?"

CONNECTING

Jessica shook her head. "Right now God is all I've got to hang on to. He's not the one doing this to me—He's the one who's getting me through this. This is the devil's work—and if it weren't for God, I'd be a basket case right now."

I don't envy one moment of Jessica's horrible summer, or any of the scars she still bears today. But I do envy her faith. I would love to be that sure of God, to hold to Him that securely. Instead, when trouble or tragedy strikes (and compared to Jessica, I've had a pretty easy ride), my first response is always to question God. I turn back to those Old Testament promises about how if you were faithful to God, your crops would grow and your land would be fruitful, conveniently ignoring Jesus' New Testament assurance that in this world we will have tribulation.

I pray that my faith won't ever be tested as Jessica's was. But I know that God gives me no guarantees. Or rather, He does guarantee one thing: not that I "might" or "could" have tribulation, but that I "will" have it.

Jessica and I have been friends for years, and I know many observers probably think I have the stronger faith of the two of us. Over the years her church attendance hasn't always been consistent, and I'm much more likely to be found up front in church, taking an office or leading out in a program. Just goes to show how different the inward and outward measures can be. In my eyes (and, I think, in God's) Jessica is a giant-killing warrior of faith, while I'm barely able to pick up my five smooth stones—and I'm not sure where I laid my slingshot.

My only confidence lies in the fact that a needy, faith-challenged man in the Bible once told Jesus, "I believe; help my unbelief." That was good enough for Jesus. I'm hoping it still is.

These things I have spoken to you, that in Me you may have peace. In the world you will have tribulation; but be of good cheer, I have overcome the world. John 16:33, NKJV.

"Things Can't Get Any Worse"

Peace I leave with you; my peace I give you.
I do not give to you as the world gives.
Do not let your hearts be troubled and
do not be afraid. John 14:27, NIV.

I do believe; help me overcome my unbelief!
Mark 9:24, NIV.

THINK IT THROUGH

1. How do you balance God's promises of protection and blessing with the reality that "you will have tribulation"?

2. How is God's peace different from the world's peace? What kind of peace could you have in a situation like Jessica's?

3. How does God help us overcome unbelief when we face a situation that's too tough for our faith?

8.

"WISH YOU WERE HERE"

Ted wasn't the most popular guy in his graduating class. He had a few good friends, but he was fairly reserved and wasn't usually the center of attention. He preferred quieter hobbies. He liked to work with his hands. He was close to his family.

Like a lot of recent high school graduates, Ted wasn't yet entirely sure what he wanted to do with his life. He dreamed of becoming a pilot, but the high cost of flying lessons had put that dream on hold for a while. In the meantime, he worked. He had a girlfriend. He liked to help elderly people and seemed to have a special gift for relating to them.

One evening, driving home from camp meeting, Ted rolled his truck. The police said later he probably lost control of the vehicle, perhaps swerving to get back on the road after his tires had strayed onto the gravel shoulder. The truck flipped several times, landing in a ditch. Ted and his mother were inside. His mom had minor injuries; Ted died instantly.

Like the rest of his fellow church members, I froze in shock when I heard the news on the phone a few hours later. Phones across town buzzed all evening as church members shared the horrible news and updated one another on how Ted's mom was doing, how his sister was taking the shock. Over and over we said, "I can't believe it."

Twenty-one years old. Life barely beginning. A hideous accident; a tragic waste.

"Wish You Were Here"

Another level of tragedy became clear to me the next evening, as I went to the funeral home for the wake. Finding a parking place was hopeless; I parked about a block away and walked down. The front door was open, and small groups of people spilled out into the parking lot, talking, shaking their heads still in stunned disbelief.

I recognized almost every face. Two other families besides Ted's were mourning in the same funeral home that night, but it was Ted's wake that drew more than 200 people. Every member of our church, coworkers of his mom and dad, his sister's friends, Adventists from other churches in the area who had been at camp meeting when the tragedy occurred. And, most overwhelming to me, Ted's own friends and his former schoolmates.

Two years had passed since his high school graduation. Not only was every member of the graduating class there; almost everyone who had been in school a couple years ahead of Ted or behind him was there. People he'd been close to, people who'd barely known him, even a few he'd never gotten along with. It was like an academy reunion, there in the hallways and parking lot of the funeral home. A reunion without the joy. Even while people smiled and brought each other up-to-date on their lives, no one could forget why there were together.

The same crowd showed up at the church the next day for the funeral service, and most came to the graveside as well. And as I looked at face after face, shadowed by tears and pain, I thought over and over, *Ted, I wish you were here.*

I wish you'd been here, Ted, to see how many people cared about you. How many people felt a void in their lives when you were gone. How many people wanted to hug your sister and your mother and share a tiny fraction of their unimaginable pain. How many people . . .

It struck me that there was nothing—absolutely nothing—else Ted could have done in his life that would have drawn as huge and diverse a crowd as he drew by dying. It sounds harsh to say it, but it's true—about Ted and about all of us. You can get a good crowd out to your wedding, but you won't get your former enemies, your casual acquaintances. People don't come together to celebrate the way they do to mourn. Nothing except death makes us drop every-thing and say, "Hey! This person was important! He mattered!" Nothing but death makes us say, "My own dislike of her, my jeal-ousy, our quarrel, was so unimportant in the long run. I want to for-get about it—I want to show her that, deep down, I really cared."

I guess that's why we so often wish the dead person could come back and be a silent spectator at his or her own funeral. When else will you hear people get up and make speeches about what a great person you were? When else will you see your enemies, your friends, and that guy who sat across from you in calculus and never got your name right, all united in their total concern for and inter-est in *you?*

It makes me want to run around shaking everyone—including myself—and yelling, "What's wrong with us? Why can we put dif-ferences aside, show our love, acknowledge someone's importance, only when it's *too late?*"

There has to be another way. Maybe everyone should get one day dedicated especially to them—a kind of prefuneral. A day when there's simply no other purpose but just to celebrate and delight in you and all that you are. Attendance would be compulsory for ev-eryone who's ever known you, even slightly. And only good atti-tudes would be allowed in the door.

Of course, it wouldn't work. Without the shock of sudden death to jar our senses, we wouldn't show up. Or if we did, we'd take our pettiness and jealousies with us: "What's the big deal with him? How come he gets all this? The decorations for my Exclusive Celebration Day weren't nearly as elaborate as these!"

As usual, my grand schemes to change the world won't work, because I can't get the world to cooperate. As usual, the only per-son I can change is me, and that only by God's grace. With His power, I want to look at people a little differently. Maybe it's mor-bid to ask, "How would I feel about this person if she died in a car crash tomorrow?" But perhaps that's the only way I'll ever put things in perspective. Maybe that's what it'll take for me to realize that that quarrel should be put aside, that those encouraging words should be spoken, that that hug shouldn't be held back.

I'll try, I really will. But still, Ted, I wish you could have been there. We'll tell you about it when we see you again.

You sweep men away in the sleep of death;
they are like the new grass of the morning—
though in the morning it springs up new,
by evening it is dry and withered.
Psalm 90:5, 6, NIV.

THINK IT THROUGH

1. Has the fact that "life is short" made any real impact on you and on your relationships yet? If so, how?

2. Can you think of one person toward whom you would change your attitude if he or she died suddenly? Can you do anything to improve that relationship today?

3. What words of love, appreciation, or encouragement have you left unsaid in your relationships with friends and family? Choose one person today to whom you'll say those things.

ENEMIES

I couldn't start thinking about a book that centered on relationships without including the not-so-good relationships—the relationships we have with those people we just don't get along well with.

It's probably no coincidence that several of these stories deal with roommates. Roommates share an interesting, sometimes odd, relationship. Sharing living space with someone you aren't either related to or in love with is more likely to happen during your late teens or early 20s than at any other time in life. Whether it's a best friend you chose to room with and then found out how little you really had in common, or the total stranger you got stuck with through the dean's office or a newspaper advertisement, the roommate relationship is full of pitfalls. Which is probably why it's also so full of opportunities for learning and growing—even through the quarrels and slammed doors!

Whether it's a roommate, a coworker, a classmate, a boss, or a neighbor, each of us has a few people in our lives we just don't click well with. These stories are all about those kind of people—and what we can learn from, or in spite of, them. In some of these stories everything works out and people become friends afterward. In others that doesn't happen. Kind of like life. There's no guarantee we're going to like everybody, hang out with everybody, add everybody to our circle of close friends. There is, however, that sometimes-inconvenient commandment: we have to *love* everybody. I read that as meaning "Treat everyone lovingly; treat them with care and respect, no matter what your feelings will be." I trust God's Spirit to supply the feelings, if I'm open to allowing that to happen. And you know what? Most of the time He does.

9.

OPERATION LOVE LISA

During Joanne's first year at university, she shared a house with four other girls, all Christians. Within a few weeks everyone began having problems with one of the girls, Lisa. Unlike the other girls, Lisa was a new Christian, and she wasn't easy to get along with. She was selfish, unreasonable, and made sarcastic comments that left the others feeling putdown.

One evening when Lisa was out of the house Joanne and her other three housemates called a conference. "We're all more mature Christians, and she's a new believer," they pointed out. "We can help her with this attitude problem. We're just going to love the bad attitude right out of her!"

It sounded like a great plan. The four girls sealed their agreement with prayer. They were going to love Lisa until she changed her attitude.

So "Operation Love Lisa" began. Whenever Lisa behaved selfishly or made a cutting comment, the others went out of their way to be as sweet and cheerful as possible to her. No one told her that they had a problem with her critical attitude or self-centered ways. When Lisa borrowed things without permission and didn't return them, when she bad-mouthed one of the girls to another, when she played her music at top volume while they studied, when she got angry and yelled at them—they simply tried to treat her as nicely as they possibly could.

CONNECTING

The problem was, things didn't improve. Lisa continued to be a pain, while her housemates continued to treat her with Christian kindness—all the while complaining about her behind her back.

Near the end of the school year Joanne went to hear a presentation by a Christian speaker. He talked about authenticity, about how important it was to be real and genuine with others. From his own experience he shared how he had discovered that he needed to tell other people they were hurting him. "Otherwise," he said, "they would never have known they mattered enough to have any influence on my life."

His words brought Joanne to a shattering realization. For an entire year she'd acted as though nothing Lisa did mattered. "I realized that I'd been making it seem to Lisa as though she had no impact on my life whatsoever," Joanne said later. "She knew she had been mean to me, and by putting up my 'Christian' front I'd given her only the impression that there was nothing she could do to hurt me, that her life was so irrelevant to me that I could handle complete tension in our relationship."

After all, if someone is totally irrelevant to us, if we really don't care about them at all, it is fairly easy to ignore their rudeness and unkindness. That's all we're doing—ignoring it. Ignoring them. We can dress it up as "Christian love," like Joanne and her housemates did, but really all we're doing is editing that person out of our lives. Looking through or around them instead of straight at them. It's an easy way out, and if we can call it "love" we get the added bonus of feeling good about ourselves as Christians.

Real love is a lot harder. Real love means that everyone matters. You can't just ignore people or the things they do. Real love means caring enough about someone to be real with them.

Jesus was real. The four Gospels give us a variety of portraits of Jesus—the gentle friend of children, the stern rebuker of Pharisees, the easygoing guy who hung out with sinners at their parties, the whip-wielding avenger clearing out the Temple, the compassionate teacher forgiving the woman caught in adultery. What we never see is Jesus putting up a front. Jesus being fake. Jesus pretending to be something He wasn't. He told people what He thought and what

He felt. Every relationship mattered enough to Him to be real.

And real relationships involve confrontation. Before we can say, "I forgive you," we sometimes have to say, "You hurt me." If the hurt isn't real, how can the forgiveness be real? And if our love is real, how can we stand to see the person we love continue with destructive attitudes and behavior?

David Augsburger wrote a powerful book called *Caring Enough to Confront*. In it he writes, "I love you. If I love you I must tell you the truth. I want your love. I want your truth. Love me enough to tell me the truth."*

Love me enough to tell me the truth. That's not easy. That's asking for a depth and honesty in our relationships that a lot of us don't want to get into—especially with the people we don't like, the people who make us uncomfortable. But could it be that when Jesus said, "Love your enemies," He meant something more than "Put up with your enemies" or "Put on a smiley face and act nice to your enemies"?

Proverbs 27:6 tells us, "Faithful are the wounds of a friend, but the kisses of an enemy are deceitful" (NKJV). If you're my friend, I can handle your loving wounds—in fact, I need them in order to grow spiritually. Though it may hurt, I can deal with someone who really cares telling me, "You're way off track here. You need to deal with this problem in your life." What I can't learn from, what I can't grow from, is someone whose fake "kisses"—or smiles—show that they really couldn't care less about me.

In Ephesians 4:15 Paul expresses his hope that as Christians "speaking the truth in love, we will in all things grow up into him who is the Head, that is, Christ" (NIV). Speaking the truth in love. That's a high ideal to follow.

We tend to go off on one of two extremes with this caring-enough-to-confront business—maybe depending on our personality types. Either we shrink from confrontation—and thus from real, honest relationships—and hide behind the "nice Christian" mask, or else we grab our flaming swords and stride into people's lives like avenging angels, ready to point out their every flaw and shortcoming.

Paul has the answer. Speak the truth—in love. Truth without love is harsh and soul-crushing. Love without truth is fake. It's not an easy balance. We may spend a lifetime learning it. But if we're trying, if we're struggling toward that ideal in our relationships, we're going to grow. And we're going to help others grow.

What about Lisa and Joanne? Joanne did take an opportunity to talk to Lisa—honestly—before Lisa moved out at the end of the school year. She apologized for the insincerity in their relationship. "But I still feel to this day as though I let her down because I couldn't be real," Joanne says. "All I needed to do was let her know that I cared about her enough to want our relationship to be better. I know now that just as Jesus was real with everyone in His life, I need to be willing to be lovingly real with the people I care about."

Lovingly real. It doesn't sound easy, but I want that too.

> **We will no longer be infants, tossed back and forth by the waves, and blown here and there by every wind of teaching and by the cunning and craftiness of men in their deceitful scheming. Instead, speaking the truth in love, we will in all things grow up into him who is the Head, that is, Christ. From him the whole body, joined and held together by every supporting ligament, grows and builds itself up in love, as each part does its work. Ephesians 4:14-16, NIV.**

THINK IT THROUGH

1. Do you agree that honesty is an essential part of being a "grown-up" Christian? Why or why not?

2. Are there times when dishonesty is justified in the name of Christian love?

3. Is there someone in your life you need to be more authentic with? someone to whom you need to speak the truth in love?

---

*David Augsburger, *Caring Enough to Confront* (Ventura, Calif.: Regal Books, 1986), p. 8.

10.

"THAT TEACHER NO GOOD!"

Sara was spending a year as a student missionary on a Pacific island. She taught grades 1 through 4 in the little school, and the lack of resources amazed her. She thought of the classrooms of her own childhood, in which each desk had its stack of clean new textbooks, in which each child had her own exercise books and workbooks—and the teacher bought fresh worksheets each day. It seemed like a distant paradise.

Sara's classroom had only a few mismatched, battered textbooks—never enough for every child in every subject. She could make up creative, interesting worksheets for the children to do—but she had no access to a photocopier or even an old-fashioned duplicating machine to run them off. There were no charts, no workbooks, no bulletin board displays. Sara's teaching tools were limited to two blackboards at the front of the room.

The principal—who was also the pastor's wife—told Sara at the beginning of the year that she should use one blackboard to write up a permanent class schedule, indicating which grades would study which class at what time. Sara went back to her classroom, tried it, and then erased it in frustration. Writing up that schedule had just used up half her classroom resources. She *needed* both those blackboards. Besides, she discovered as the days and weeks went on that her multigrade classroom didn't work well with a fixed schedule. She liked to be a little more flexible, sometimes allowing one class to run longer when needed, or merging two classes together.

The principal was irritated every time she walked into Sara's classroom. Several times she mentioned how important it was to have a schedule on the board. Sara tried to explain her reasons for not having one, but that just annoyed the principal more. Sara just shrugged and decided not to let it bother her. She and the principal just had different management styles, that was all. Besides, Sara had already noticed that the principal wasn't very popular with students, with other teachers, or indeed with the church members. She had an abrupt, almost rude manner that put people off. Sara wasn't too concerned about getting on her good side.

One day, while Sara was in the middle of a Bible lesson with her children, the door opened, and the principal strode into the room. She glanced around Sara's classroom and began loudly criticizing several things Sara was doing wrong.

Sara couldn't believe it. Her boss was chewing her out—in front of the students? From what she knew about teaching, that was supposed to be a *huge* no-no. Staff were always supposed to support each other when students were around, no matter how they might disagree privately.

Then the principal's eye fell on the blackboard—covered with fill-in-the-blank exercises Sara had written up for her students. "And this!" the woman said, pointing an accusing finger. "How many times have I told you that that blackboard is for you to write your schedule on? But no—you won't follow instructions. You think you know everything! And of course, why would you need to write up a schedule? You don't even *follow* a schedule in here—you just do what you want, when you want! I pity the teacher who has these students next year, when you're back in the States! She'll have to teach them everything over again, because they certainly haven't learned anything this year!"

With one last contemptuous glance around the room, the principal turned and strode out, slamming the door behind her.

"That Teacher No Good!"

An eerie silence hung in the air after she left. Sara, who could feel the blood flushing her cheeks, didn't even want to look the children in the eyes. What must they think?

She found out what they thought, quickly and bluntly. One third-grade boy pointed at the door where the principal had been and said angrily, "That teacher no good!" Then he paused, with a questioning look, and said, "Crazy?"

The other students chimed in, adding uncomplimentary comments about the principal. Everything confirmed what Sara already knew—nobody had any respect for the woman.

Sara dismissed her students for recess and sat at her desk, thinking about what to do. She had tried so many times to talk to the principal herself, but she just couldn't communicate with the woman. But this was a real problem. Sara wasn't too concerned for herself. The school year was ending, and soon she'd be gone forever. But for the people left behind—the students, the church members, the community—the principal's attitude was a problem. The fact that she was the pastor's wife made it a bigger problem. The pastor was doing his best to have an effective ministry on the island, but his wife had actually alienated many people with her abrasive approach.

So Sara decided on a course of action. It wasn't an easy thing to do, but she felt it was the right thing. She talked to the pastor.

Sitting down with a man (her superior) and telling him that his wife (who was also her superior) was causing problems with her attitude was a difficult thing to do. Sara didn't know how he'd react. Wouldn't the natural response be for him to take his wife's side, to think Sara was being critical and dishonest? Sara told him about the incident in the classroom, and added, "After she left, the students made some comments that—well, that made me think they didn't respect her very much."

"What did they say?" asked the pastor. It was almost the first thing he'd said since Sara had begun.

Half wishing she hadn't gotten into this, Sara repeated the students' comments. "I've heard similar things said about your wife by others in the school and in the church," she said, swallowing the huge lump in her throat. "I think—I think it's really hurting your ministry here, Pastor."

The pastor sat quietly, his hands folded in his lap, nodding now and then as Sara spoke. He looked a little hurt, but not angry. And he didn't have much to say. When Sara had finally run out of words he simply said, "Thank you for bringing this to my attention, Sara." That was all. She left his office, wondering if she'd made things better or worse.

Sara was nervous as she approached the school the next day. Surely the pastor must have mentioned their conversation to his wife. Would she try to get revenge on Sara by making their professional relationship even more miserable than it already was?

When they met with the other teachers for staff worship, the principal gave no sign that anything was wrong. In fact, she said "Hello, Sara" quite pleasantly, and greeted the other staff members more courteously than usual.

All day Sara was braced for a backlash. Instead she saw something quite different. She saw the principal actually, visibly, change her ways. She was obviously making an effort to be more polite, more civil, to everybody—including the students.

Near the end of the year Sara sat on the playground and watched as the principal joined some of the younger children in a game. As they ran off the playing field, two of the little girls were holding her hands—a sight Sara couldn't have imagined a few months earlier. It took such a slight change in the principal's behavior to evoke a response from the children.

When Sara left for the year, the principal gave her a warm handshake and said she would miss her—and actually sounded sincere! Sara was impressed. Here was a woman who had taken a rebuke to heart and honestly allowed God's Spirit to work in her life. She was impressed with the pastor, too. Sara guessed he must have used an incredibly tactful approach to deal with the issue without hurting his wife.

For almost a year Sara had been trying to do the "Christian" thing—to ignore the principal's behavior, to acquiesce to whatever unreasonable demands she made, to keep everyone happy. When she stepped out of that mold and took the unpleasant, risky step of confronting the issue, things changed—and the principal was better able to fulfill the mission God had for her to do.

Confrontation isn't easy. Knowing when to confront and when to go along is even more difficult. But, as Sara learned, there are times when nothing else will do.

> **Let a righteous man strike me—it is a kindness;**
> **let him rebuke me—it is oil on my head.**
> **My head will not refuse it. Psalm 141:5, NIV.**

> **Do not rebuke a mocker or he will hate you;**
> **rebuke a wise man and he will love you.**
> **Proverbs 9:8, NIV.**

THINK IT THROUGH

1. Compare this story to Joanne's experience with Lisa in "Operation Love Lisa." Was Sara in a different situation because the principal was her superior rather than her equal? Do the same rules about caring confrontation apply in both situations?

2. How do we know where to draw the line between Christian confrontation and an unchristian attitude of complaint and criticism?

3. How do you handle being on the receiving end of confrontation or "rebuke"?

11.

AN UNHAPPY LIFE

This is another story about Sara's year as a student missionary. Based on these two stories alone, you might think Sara did nothing but make enemies that year, but in fact she had quite a good year. Maybe it's just that the difficult experiences are the ones we learn the most from.

The mission where she worked was growing exponentially, and Sara and her fellow SMs—three guys and two other girls—were busy nearly all the time. Sara seemed to enjoy the company of the guys more than of the girls. Like her, the three guys threw themselves wholeheartedly into the cross-cultural experience. They got to know local friends and visited in their homes, attended events in the community, planned extracurricular activities for their students, and were busy in the local church.

The other two female student missionaries, Rachel and Gina, were less outgoing. They came from the same college and had been friends before arriving in the mission field, and even after several months they still mostly stuck together. They seemed timid and shy, and unwilling to get involved enthusiastically in the mission and in the community.

Sara didn't have problems getting along with either Rachel or Gina, but it annoyed her that whenever something was going on, these two girls would hang back, wait to be invited, and need to be reassured that they were really wanted. "Stop worrying about them!" she told the three guys one night when Rachel and Gina had decided not to come out with them to a friend's house in the community. "They're just boring people—they like to whine and complain. I'm not going to spend this whole year baby-sitting them."

Then, over spring break, four of the student missionaries had the opportunity to travel to another island for a vacation—Sara, Rachel, and two of the guys, Jared and Chad. Jared's mom was able to join them and enjoyed meeting her son's coworkers.

Sara enjoyed the break from work and the opportunity to visit yet another country. She didn't pay much attention to Rachel until one evening when Sara happened to end up walking on the beach with Jared's mother.

"How are things going over there with your work?" Jared's mom wanted to know.

"It's going great," Sara said. "We're having a great year. We're really busy."

"I wonder if everyone is having a good year," the woman said. "I've noticed how unhappy Rachel seems. She seems like the kind of person who's not going to have a very happy life."

She's not going to have a happy life. The words resonated in Sara's head. She couldn't stop thinking about them as she looked at Rachel the following day. How tragic to be 20 years old and to have someone who had just met you already predicting you were going to have an unhappy life!

Sara made time the next evening to take another walk along the beach—this time with Rachel. For the first time she began to really talk with the other girl about the year of experiences they were sharing—how Rachel liked the island, her job, the student missionary life. The whole evening was an eye-opener for Sara.

"Sometimes I wish I was more like you and the guys," Rachel admitted. "You're so outgoing, so lively. I'm just not like that. It's easier for me just to stick with Gina and do things with her. Maybe I've even held her back from getting involved a bit. But I'm just not the kind of person who gets out and meets new people easily. You guys are leaders. I'm not a leader."

"Well, anyone can learn to be more outgoing," Sara said.

CONNECTING

"Maybe," said Rachel. "But my background is very different from yours. I was taught that people—girls, especially—should be quiet and unassuming. Not loud, not bold or forward. In some ways I really admire the way you act, but I was taught not to behave that way."

As they talked Sara understood a lot more about where Rachel was coming from. On the surface both girls looked similar—white skin, brown hair, Caucasian features. In the "foreign" world of the Pacific island where they worked, Sara had just assumed that she and all the other SMs were basically "the same," while the islanders were different. Now she understood that Rachel came from a culture very different from hers. Rachel's immigrant parents valued hard work, respect, and a sober, quiet demeanor. Strong-willed, assertive young women had never been Rachel's role models.

Sara took a new perspective back to the island with her after spring break. Now that she and Rachel had talked, now that she understood the cultural differences between them a little more, she saw so many ways in which she had cut Rachel—and Gina, too—out of her activities. She had shrugged them aside, failed to respect the ways in which they were different from her, assumed that they couldn't be her friends if they didn't fit her idea of how they should act.

Did Rachel go on to live an unhappy life? Sara doesn't know . . . they haven't kept in touch. Sara and Rachel didn't become best friends. Rachel didn't suddenly become outgoing and assertive. But for the rest of that year they were friends. Sara had more respect for Rachel—Rachel as herself, not as Sara wanted her to be. Understanding where she was coming from made the difference, as it so often does.

There is neither Jew nor Greek, slave nor free, male nor female, for you are all one in Christ Jesus. Galatians 3:28, NIV.

An Unhappy Life

1. Does "all one in Christ Jesus" mean that we need to be more, or less, aware of cultural differences between ourselves and other people? Do such differences really matter?

2. Is there anyone in your life whom you are trying to shape into *your* idea of what they should be? How would the relationship be different if you accepted that person as he or she is? Is that always possible?

12.

"NEVER MIND"

My college roommate drove me insane.

Not all the time, mind you. Usually we got along fairly well. But like every roommate, she had a couple habits that sent me right around the bend. One of them was her use of the phrase "Never mind."

Now, college was a culturally broadening experience for me to start with. I had grown up in St. John's, Newfoundland, Canada, a place that didn't feature a lot of ethnic diversity. Arriving on the campus of Andrews University was an eye-opener in terms of meeting people of different races and cultures.

My roommate was from Thailand. My cousin, who had spent a year in Thailand as a student missionary, said that Pree's annoying habit of saying "Never mind" whenever I tried to explain or discuss something was typical of Thai people she had met. "They think it's rude to argue," she told me. "It's considered more polite just to ignore the problem, not talk about it."

One day things went too far. The dorm mailboxes were in the basement of the building, and on my way to class I checked the box and found a letter for me and two for Pree. Since I wasn't planning to go back to the room for at least four or five hours, I left hers in the box, figuring she'd get them sooner by checking the box herself.

That evening I asked if she'd gotten the two letters.

"No," she said in her slightly accented English. "I got two letters?"

"Never Mind"

"Yeah, I saw them there on my way to class this morning, but I left them for you to pick up."

"Oh." There was a long pause; then she went downstairs and came back with her mail. She sat looking through it and sighed heavily.

"Why you didn't bring my letters up for me?" she asked at last.

"What? Oh, uh, I would've, but I was on my way to class and—"

"It's OK. Never mind." Another heavy sigh. "I just thought you would bring them up for me."

"No, you see, it's like I said, I was going to class and—"

"Never mind." Sigh.

I put aside my book and sat up. "Look Pree, I'm sorry. I didn't bring them up because I thought you—"

"No. Never mind."

Silence continued for some time while I tried to go back to studying. Every so often she would let out another deep sigh and a whispered comment. "Some people . . . so selfish. Not even to bring my letters up. Sooo selfish . . ."

Yet every time I tried to explain, she cut me off. "Never mind."

At this point I decided we were getting beyond cultural differences and into personality problems. She wanted to continue to make me feel bad about not bringing her mail up. But she didn't want to give me a chance to explain myself.

For most of us, especially extremely verbal people like me, being denied the chance to state your case, to explain yourself, is one of the most frustrating things that can happen. It reminds me of an episode of a sitcom I saw recently in which one character teaches another how to deflect negative comments by simply staring off into space and saying "Whatever" to any comment the other person makes. Not getting a response drives us crazy!

What about God? Does God give us a chance to explain ourselves, to state our case? Or does His omnipotence mean we haven't even got the right to talk back? Perhaps as novelist Caryl Rivers suggests when one of her characters considers talking back to the Almighty, He'll just respond by turning us into pillars of salt: "I Am who I Am, and you are *salt*. Zap!"

A little while ago I heard a preacher suggest that when Jesus said on the cross, "My God, why have You forsaken Me?" He was the only person in the world who had the right to ask God "Why?" Jesus could do it, but none of the rest of us can.

I think I disagree just a little with that preacher's conclusion. Yes, I agree that Jesus, as the Son of God, was the only one who had the right to put that question to His heavenly Father. But even though the rest of us don't have any right to question God, to talk back to Him, He allows us to anyway. When we stand up to start complaining to God, making our case, asking questions, He doesn't blast us into a pillar of salt. He doesn't even turn away with a frustrating "Never mind."

He listens. He allows us to talk. And He answers.

If you've taken even a casual stroll through the book of Psalms, you'll find this conclusion unavoidable. God allowed the writers and editors of the Psalms to fill up a pretty large chunk of the book with complaints—complaints that enemies were attacking, that trouble was coming, and that God wasn't doing enough to help! King David and his fellow psalmists weren't always happy with the way God was running the universe, and they didn't mind putting their complaints down in writing and setting them to music. Not only did God *not* strike them dead—He saved their whines and moans as part of our Scriptures. That says something to me about His willingness to listen, to let us talk.

Job was another great talker. He *knew* he didn't deserve the bad luck heaped upon him, even though his friends assured him he was being punished for his sins. He talked back. He argued his case before the Almighty. "If only I knew where to find [God]; if only I could go to his dwelling! I would state my case before him and fill my mouth with arguments" (Job 23:3, 4, NIV).

Even in the middle of terrible suffering, in the face of God's inexplicable silence, Job remained convinced that if he could just state his case before the Almighty, God would listen. Job would "fill his mouth with arguments" and present them before God. He didn't expect to hear God say, "Never mind."

Job's ringing declaration of faith in God: "Though He slay me, yet will I trust Him" is followed immediately with "Even so, I will defend my own ways before Him" (Job 13:15, NKJV). Job's unshakable trust is in a God who will allow him to speak, who will hear what he has to say.

And God does allow Job to speak. Not only Job, but his misguided and unhelpful friends are allowed to say whatever's on their mind for 36 chapters before God talks back.

When God talks to Job, He doesn't explain the reason behind Job's suffering. Instead He hits Job with a series of questions that basically add up to: "Who are you to question Me? Did you create the world? Do you understand how it works? Could you do My job?" There's not much Job could say in reply to that except "Uh, no—sorry I bothered You."

In fact, what Job does say is "Surely I spoke of things I did not understand, things too wonderful for me to know" (Job 42:3, NIV). Job accepts God's judgment—that an ordinary human being like Job, like you and me, simply hasn't got the capacity to understand the big answers to the big questions.

But God doesn't strike Job dead for daring to ask. Instead He commends Job, rewards him, restores him. Apparently it's possible to question God and still please Him. We are far too limited to enter into a debate with God, yet He doesn't turn away when we ask and argue. He listens. He allows us to speak.

So when you've seen injustice and tragedy, when you've struggled with questions you don't have answers to, when you've wanted to howl and rage at the unfairness and stupidity of life, take it to God. Go outside under the dark night sky and howl to Him. He's there. He's listening. And He'll never say, "Never mind."

If only I knew where to find [God]; if only I could go to his dwelling! I would state my case before him and fill my mouth with arguments. I would find out what he would answer me, and consider what he would say. Would he oppose me with great power? No, he would not press charges against me. There an upright man could present

**his case before him, and I would be delivered
forever from my
judge. Job 23:3-7, NIV.**

THINK IT THROUGH

1. If you could state your case before God right now, what complaints or questions would you have to bring to Him? Have you "stated your case" in prayer? If not, what holds you back from saying these things to God?

2. How do you think God would respond to you?

3. Is there a positive way to communicate with a fellow human being who doesn't allow you to explain yourself?

13.

THE WRONG ROOM

Nancy was returning for her junior year in college. When she arrived at the dorm with her luggage and checked in at the desk, bad news awaited.

"Sorry, but you didn't reserve your room at the end of last school year," the dean's assistant told her, checking a list. "That room is no longer available."

"What? Of course I reserved my room. I've had the same room ever since my freshman year."

"I'm sorry, but I don't have your name on the list. That room has already been assigned to another student, and she's already moved in."

Nancy was furious. She wasted a lot of time in the dean's office arguing about the mix-up, but at the end of a long, hot afternoon the answer was no different. "Her" room was gone; someone else was living there. Nancy had to move to a room at the end of a remote, dark corridor on the older side of the dorm.

She wasn't one bit happy.

All year Nancy couldn't shake the feeling she was living in the wrong room. Every time she walked down the corridor past her old room she felt a stab of jealousy. It didn't help when she found out that her old room had been given to an incoming freshman. The freshman girl, Angie, seemed like a nice enough kid, but she certainly didn't deserve Nancy's room, and Nancy was prepared to dislike her on sight.

CONNECTING

At the end of that year Nancy was careful to go to the dean's office and make it very clear that she and her best friend wanted to reserve a particular room—not her old room, but another bright, pleasant, conveniently located room in the new wing of the dorm. Nancy felt a little more secure about her rooming situation as she headed home that summer.

On the first day of her senior year Nancy found herself, unbelievably, starring in a repeat performance of the previous year's dorm fiasco. "But I reserved the room!" she shouted, a half dozen times, at the poor harassed girl behind the desk. "You *must* have the sheet! I signed it right here in this office!"

But her reservation had been lost again. And there was more bad news. The friend she'd planned to room with had decided that very day that she wasn't coming back to college. Nancy had no room and no roommate.

"But there's a nice room we can put you in," the dean's assistant assured her. "Angie Evans needs a roommate—she's a sophomore, but I'm sure you'll get along fine. Do you know her?"

Nancy couldn't believe it. This was the very same Angie who had stolen her room the year before. This was the girl she'd spent an entire year secretly hating. Now she was being forced to room with her.

This time Nancy went to the top—she spoke with the dean herself. But it was no use. At the end of the day she found herself assigned to Angie's room.

The roommate relationship started off on the wrong foot, to say the least. That evening, when Nancy started trying to hang her posters, things got worse. Angie already had very clear ideas about how to decorate the room, and they didn't merge well with Nancy's at all. They ended up dividing the room clearly in half, with Angie's unicorns and stuffed animals on her side, and Nancy's artsy poster prints and IKEA lamps on her side. The room looked like it suffered from multiple personality disorder.

The next morning Angie bounded out of bed at 6:00 a.m. and began singing loudly and cheerfully while she showered, tidied her side of the room, and got her clothes ready for the day. Nancy moaned and pulled a pillow over her head. Along with all her other

The Wrong Room

faults, Angie was a morning person. Could things get any worse?

Apparently they could. That evening both girls attempted to straighten out their course outlines and new textbooks. Angie got to her stereo first and switched on a country music station as she worked. To Nancy, the sound of country music was only a few notches above that of fingernails scraping on a blackboard. When Angie switched off her music and went out of the room for a few minutes, Nancy quickly turned on her radio to a classical station, and got dark looks from Angie when she returned.

Nancy was discouraged. Her whole senior year was about to be ruined by being forced to room with a perky, superficial little sophomore with whom she had absolutely nothing in common. She was tempted to visit the dean's office again and beg for a change, but she had a feeling she was already getting a reputation as a troublemaker, so she kept quiet.

A week later, when Nancy began to tidy and clean the room for Sabbath, she expected more trouble from Angie. In three years of college she'd never had a roommate who liked things as clean as she did. She was used to picking up after messy roommates.

But to her surprise, Angie pitched in enthusiastically, scrubbing the shower while Nancy cleaned the sink and toilet. When they had borrowed, used, and returned the vacuum cleaner, both girls sat back on their beds and enjoyed the glowing, clean look of the room. It was the first moment of camaraderie they'd shared.

As the weeks went on, Nancy found she also appreciated Angie's study habits. She had lived with roommates who wanted to listen to music while they studied, or who studied loudly with friends in the room, or who never seemed to study at all. But Angie, like Nancy, settled down at her desk for a couple quiet hours in the evening and didn't want to be disturbed. It made studying easier and gave Nancy a break from the otherwise endless country music.

One evening after about two hours of studying, Angie said, "I'm going out to get a snack. Do you want me to bring you back something?"

"Well, what I'd really like is some Chinese food, but . . ."

"That's great! That's exactly what I want too! Why don't I run down to the takeout place and bring some back for both of us? Steamed rice and spring rolls OK?"

"My favorite," said Nancy.

Later, as they both wielded their chopsticks and enjoyed their snack, Nancy and Angie had their first real talk. They found they could make each other laugh—they shared the same offbeat sense of humor.

The country music and the unicorns didn't fade away, but Nancy began to appreciate the roommate she'd been so reluctant to have. A real friendship grew, based on a few common tastes and expanding to include so much more.

Now, with college days long behind her, Nancy says, "Of all my college friends, Angie is the one I've stayed closest to. If you keep an open mind, you'll find friendship in unexpected places."

On one occasion an expert in the law stood up to test Jesus. "Teacher," he asked, "what must I do to inherit eternal life?" "What is written in the Law?" he replied. "How do you read it?" He answered: " 'Love the Lord your God with all your heart and with all your soul and with all your strength and with all your mind' "; and, " 'Love your neighbor as yourself.' " "You have answered correctly," Jesus replied. "Do this and you will live." But he wanted to justify himself, so he asked Jesus, "And who is my neighbor?" In reply Jesus said: "A man was going down from Jerusalem to Jericho, when he fell into the hands of robbers. They stripped him of his clothes, beat him and went away, leaving him half dead. A priest happened to be going down the same road, and . . . he passed by on the other side. So too, a Levite . . . passed by on the other side. But a Samaritan . . . took pity on him. He went to him

and bandaged his wounds. . . . Then he . . . took him to an inn and took care of him. . . . Which of these three do you think was a neighbor to the man who fell into the hands of robbers?"
The expert in the law replied, "The one who had mercy on him." Jesus told him, "Go and do likewise." Luke 10:25-37, NIV.

THINK IT THROUGH

1. How often do we allow superficial differences or imagined injuries to erect barriers between ourselves and other people?

2. Have you ever found a good friend in an unexpected place?

14.

THE POWER OF HATE

Valerie and Christine were friends—once. Something went wrong. Christine betrayed a trust—at least that's how it seemed to Valerie. Valerie was furious. When she went to Christine to confront her and try to straighten things out, Christine insisted that Valerie had it all wrong. "You're the one with the problem, not me!" she said. They ended up shouting at each other.

The next time they ran into each other—they worked in the same building—each looked the opposite way. Their mutual friends quickly learned not to invite them over on the same evening. In fact, friends learned not even to mention Christine's name around Valerie. Valerie was very much the "injured party" in the whole deal, and she couldn't stand even to talk about Christine—unless it was to rehash, once again, how much Christine had hurt her and what a terrible person she was. And her friends got tired of hearing that after a while.

Valerie spent a lot of time thinking about Christine and how unfair she'd been. She'd lie awake wondering how someone who was supposed to be a friend could have treated her that way. Her anger began to turn to hate. She couldn't think of a single nice thing about this woman whose company she had once enjoyed.

If Valerie arrived at a party or a meeting and saw that Christine was there, she turned around and left. Afterward she'd sit outside in her car, fuming, wondering how all those other people could still stand to have Christine around, to invite her out and include her. Didn't they know what kind of person she was?

One day Valerie was driving home from work. As she came to an intersection she saw Christine's car approaching from the opposite direction. She couldn't even see Christine herself yet—just the familiar outline of her vehicle. That was enough to set Valerie's anger rising again. She could understand why people said anger "made your blood boil"—she could actually feel her rage toward Christine coursing through her veins, filling her body. She turned her face away as their cars passed. Even a glimpse of Christine might be enough to send her over the edge.

In the moments after Christine's car passed, Valerie's anger ebbed. It didn't leave completely—it never did. Any sight or mention of Christine was enough to trigger it, but it was always there, a constant undercurrent to Valerie's life.

Suddenly, as if her vision had cleared for just one moment, a thought pierced Valerie's mind. It was a simple one: *Christine is ruining my life.*

Hadn't Christine already ruined her life with her unkindness? *Well, to be honest,* Valerie thought, *she hasn't really.* She had done a lot of damage, but time had passed, and the direct fallout from that incident was pretty well over and forgotten. Yet something remained—the anger, the hatred.

She revised her revelation: *My anger at Christine is ruining my life.*

That was the reality, though she didn't like the implication. It meant that her unhappiness, her frayed nerves, her edginess, were not really Christine's fault at all. They were Valerie's own responsibility. She was choosing to hang on to bitterness rather than to forgive. And she wasn't hurting Christine very much at all—but she was destroying herself.

Valerie was a Christian. She had gone on thinking of herself as a Christian all through the Christine incident, even praying to ask God how Christine could have been so cruel, how she should deal with the problem. She had managed to ignore the very obvious solution presented all through the Gospels—love and forgive. And move on.

CONNECTING

In failing to move on, Valerie had somehow turned herself into a different person. An angry, hate-filled person. Even—she paused over the word, but then accepted it—an evil person. Evil—the terrible, destructive power of hate—had begun to take over her life. It had slipped in without her notice, and now it was controlling her, changing who she was.

Valerie found herself shaking. She was actually frightened as she realized what she had allowed to happen. At the first opportunity she pulled into a parking lot and prayed—more honestly and freely than she had in months. She confessed her own sin, her anger, her hatred. She asked for the grace to forgive and forget. "And Lord," she prayed, "give me the strength never to allow evil to have such power in my life again."

Valerie felt light. She felt free and even happy again. She felt filled with God's Spirit as she turned her car back onto the street.

With the grace to forgive and move on came, eventually, the grace to heal. Valerie and Christine became friends again. "She became," Valerie relates, "a true and trusted friend, a blessing in my life."

Anyone who claims to be in the light but hates his brother is still in the darkness. Whoever loves his brother lives in the light, and there is nothing in him to make him stumble. But whoever hates his brother is in the darkness and walks around in the darkness; he does not know where he is going, because the darkness has blinded him. 1 John 2:9-11, NIV.

In your anger do not sin: Do not let the sun go down while you are still angry, and do not give the devil a foothold. Ephesians 4:26, 27, NIV.

The Power of Hate

1. How can you deal with a truly hurtful experience without allowing your feelings to turn to hate?

2. Is it possible to heal a relationship when one person doesn't think they've done anything wrong? If so, how? If not, what's our responsibility as Christians?

3. Is there someone in your life you need to forgive? Do you need to ask God to help you move on?

15.

INNOCENCE LOST

The stories I've shared so far in this section have been about quarrels among friends, incompatible roommates, domineering bosses. Everyday conflicts that rub and irritate us like the grain of sand in the oyster—and, we hope, produce pearls of wisdom and spiritual growth. But there's a far more serious level to this idea of "people we don't get along with," and the story my friend Jeff told me is on that level. It makes the other conflicts in this section seem almost trivial by comparison—but it's a story that has to be told.

You see, sometimes our "enemies" aren't just people whose habits are a little irritating or whose outlook is different from ours or whose manner is somewhat abrasive. Occasionally in life we encounter people who are truly evil—or at least people who do truly evil things—and as Christians we somehow have to deal with that reality.

Jeff grew up in an Adventist home, in an Adventist church. Like a lot of kids, he reached his early teen years feeling a little ambivalent about the church and religion—it was part of his life, the reality he'd always known, yet he was beginning to see that there were a lot of exciting things out there in the big wide world, and not all of them were compatible with being a Seventh-day Adventist. Church, religion, and God seemed just a little boring.

Then the year Jeff was 12, Pastor Dave came to serve as youth pastor at their church, and things changed.

Pastor Dave was fresh out of college and full of new ideas.

Besides getting the older teens and the young adults active, he also revitalized the dying Pathfinder Club. Soon Jeff and his closest friends, Mike, Megan, and Tia, looked forward to the honking horn of Pastor Dave's van outside their houses as if it were the call of Gabriel's trumpet. They piled into that van for hikes, socials, camp-outs—even previously boring events such as singing at the senior citizens' home somehow seemed exciting when Pastor Dave organized them.

With Pastor Dave at the helm, Jeff's seventh- and eighth-grade years flew by, filled with action and discovery. Jeff survived his first serious crush (on Tia, who up till then had always been just "one of the gang" but who was suddenly looking much more attractive), he prepared to go away to boarding academy for ninth grade, got baptized, and started realizing that Christianity could be a lifestyle as exciting and fun as anything the world had to offer. It didn't have to be boring. Pastor Dave was living proof of that.

Then, in the summer after eighth-grade graduation, as Jeff and his friends were packing their bags for academy, the storm struck.

It began when Jeff's mom said she had to go out one night to an emergency church board meeting. She was out very late, and the next day she looked sad and serious. For the next few days Jeff's parents always seemed to be having deep conversations on the phone, dropping their voices whenever Jeff came by.

Jeff called Mike, Megan, and Tia to go out to the park with him, but only Mike and Megan showed up. "I don't know what's wrong with Tia," Megan said. "She won't come out. She said she doesn't want to go anywhere."

"Is everyone acting weird at your house?" Jeff wanted to know. "Something's going on."

"There *is* something going on," Mike said, "and it's got something to do with Tia. I don't know what it is, but I heard my folks talking, and I know they mentioned her name."

By Sabbath everyone knew. Pastor Dave had resigned. The secret had finally come out—for more than a year he'd been carrying on a sexual relationship with an underage girl, 13-year-old Tia.

Jeff couldn't believe it. No one could believe it. Pastor Dave was a hero, an idol. He was a man of God. He loved kids. How could he have entrapped a young girl in that kind of relationship?

All hell broke loose in Jeff's home church. He was glad to get away to academy to escape it. Rumors and accusations flew back and forth. Pastor Dave went away, then came back. Some people wanted him to have his job back. Some people even blamed Tia.

Tia went away to academy with the others, and she and Jeff remained close friends. She was badly scarred by the whole ordeal, but eventually she was able to talk about it. "I was scared," she said. "I mean, I was flattered and everything at first, but then, when it got to the point of actually having sex, I was scared. He told me I'd be in big trouble if anyone found out." Tia was devastated by the harsh, judgmental attitudes of some of the people in church. But slowly, far away from the scene of the crime, she began the lifelong process of healing.

Jeff was bruised too. He was so angry at Pastor Dave that he couldn't even think about the man. And he felt betrayed. He had given all his trust, all his admiration, to this man. And he'd believed Pastor Dave to be a true Christian. Everything he'd come to believe about Christians, about Christianity, about God, came into question.

He remembered sitting in church during their eighth-grade graduation service only a few months before. Pastor Dave had preached the sermon, about the importance of obeying God's law in everything they did. Jeff even remembered Pastor Dave saying the words "Thou shalt not commit adultery" and talking about the importance of keeping both your thoughts and your actions pure. Now he wanted to rewind back to that moment, stand up in church, and yell, "How can anyone be such a hypocrite?"

Time passed. Nobody gets over this kind of thing, but people move on in their own ways. Pastor Dave never got hired as a pastor again, but he stayed in the church and in the area. He found another job—not working with kids—and continued to maintain that he hadn't done wrong, that Tia had been a willing partner in their relationship.

Jeff moved through his teen years questioning God and the church. He finally decided in favor of God, but he still wasn't so sure about the church. He became a committed Christian and continued to attend the Adventist church, but he still had a lot of doubts.

Tia grew up, got married, and continued to struggle with the aftermath of Pastor Dave's abuse in her life. She also worried about other young girls, girls as innocent and trusting as she had once been. Shouldn't the church be doing more to protect girls like her, to prevent this kind of thing from happening, to make it clear that actions like Pastor Dave's were totally unacceptable?

Tia's solution, when she reached her early 20s, was to launch a lawsuit—against the church and against Dave himself. She hoped that by doing so she'd not only get some closure for herself on the whole painful incident, but she'd send a loud, clear message to the organization that she felt had allowed her to be abused and had failed to help her afterward.

One day while the lawsuit was in progress Jeff got a phone call from Pastor Dave—just Dave now. They sometimes attended the same church, and Jeff's anger against the man was still so intense he found it hard to be polite to him when they met.

What was hard for Jeff to believe was how, even as a grown man, he got scared when he got Dave's call. Dave had been a powerful force in his life, and he felt both betrayed and manipulated by him. He knew Dave wanted to discuss Tia and the court case, and he knew he wasn't going to give Dave any information that might be helpful to him. But he also felt he had to see Dave, to talk with him.

"I had to meet him," Jeff says, "not to help him with his agenda, but to be able to face this man as a man myself. I also knew this would be the only chance I would ever have to talk with him about the hurt that he had caused, not only to Tia, but also to me and many others like me who had held him up on a pedestal when we were young. When someone is such an integral part of who you are as a Christian, and then turns out to be manipulative, perhaps even evil, it affects the way you look at being a Christian. In fact, I saw him as a large reason for the anger I felt against my church."

So Jeff agreed to the meeting, and did a lot of praying in the days beforehand. He prayed for the strength to confront Dave honestly and openly, and to stand up to him without being manipulated.

Jeff's prayers were answered. From his point of view the meeting was a complete success. He was able to tell Dave everything on his mind, and when the older man attempted to manipulate him, Jeff experienced the freeing realization that he was no longer a child. He was a man, Dave's equal, able to stand up to him.

"When he said that I had to admit he had been a good youth leader," says Jeff, "I was able to tell him how his actions had tainted everything that went before. All the good that had been done, all the spiritual lessons, had been tainted by his abusive actions."

Jeff learned a lot from his meeting with Dave. He learned that with God's power, he could face and even confront the enemy who had so seriously betrayed his youthful trust. Jeff's bitterness against the church began to heal too. He realized that Dave had harmed the church itself, just as surely as he had harmed individuals. Jeff could now separate Dave's actions from Christianity, from the Adventist Church, rejecting the man while accepting the God he claimed to serve.

For Jeff, there's one more step to this process. "I still need to forgive Dave," he says. "Not for what he did to Tia—that's not mine to forgive. But I need to forgive him for the hurt he caused me. I couldn't do that at the time. I can now, and I need to speak with him again, to tell him that."

Jeff's response to this has cleared up a lot of my confusion over what forgiveness is and isn't. Forgiveness doesn't mean you have to forgive a person for an apparently unforgivable act done to someone else. Whether Tia can ever forgive Dave for abusing her is between her and God. Jeff has to struggle only with the issue of what Dave did to *him*.

Forgiveness also doesn't mean allowing the offense to happen again. Jeff is now the father of two small daughters. "I would never allow my daughters to be alone with this man," Jeff says, "and if I ever saw him placed in a position where he had any power over children or teenagers, I would do everything in my power to stop it." Dave has a sin problem that he has never fully addressed, and forgiving him doesn't mean ignoring that problem.

What forgiveness does mean is acknowledging, as Jeff says, that "my pain over this has healed." It means sharing that healing with the other person as much as you are able to do—then moving on. That doesn't happen overnight. It may not happen in a week or a month. It may take 20 years, as it has in Jeff's case. It may take a lifetime. And there are no shortcuts—we have to go right through the pain, through the anger, through the confrontation, to get to healing and forgiveness. But if we're open to it, the Spirit will get us there.

> **If an enemy were insulting me, I could endure it;**
> **if a foe were raising himself against me,**
> **I could hide from him. But it is you,**
> **a man like myself, my companion, my close**
> **friend, with whom I once enjoyed sweet**
> **fellowship as we walked with the throng at**
> **the house of God. Psalm 55:12-14, NIV.**

> **Do not take revenge, my friends,**
> **but leave room for God's wrath,**
> **for it is written: "It is mine to avenge; I will**
> **repay," says the Lord. Romans 12:19, NIV.**

> **Love your enemies, bless those who curse you,**
> **do good to those who hate you, and pray for**
> **those who spitefully use you and persecute you.**
> **Matthew 5:44, NKJV.**

THINK IT THROUGH

1. When God asks us to forgive someone else, does He expect us to do it instantly? Is it necessary to go through a healing process first, or is this just postponing our duty to forgive?

2. Is it always necessary to confront someone who has betrayed us or seriously hurt us? Can healing take place without confrontation? What if it's never possible to see or speak with that person again?

3. What is your response to Pastor Dave in this story? How do you deal with Christian leaders who betray people's trust?

4. To what extent do you hold the church responsible when you hear stories of this kind of abuse?

FAMILY

They're the most complex, important, frustrating, rewarding group of people (pick any or all adjectives that apply) you'll ever encounter in your life. They're the people whose lives will always be intricately entwined with your own, even though you had absolutely no choice about being associated with them. They're sometimes the only ones who can make you cry; they're sometimes the only ones who can dry your tears when the rest of the world turns its back.

They are, of course, your family. Your parents, brothers and sisters, grandparents, extended family—all those people who came prepackaged as part of your life.

We all know how family is supposed to work. Evolutionists will tell you that the purpose of the human family is so that vulnerable young human beings can be nurtured and cared for in a stable environment during their unusually long (compared to the animals) period of maturation. That's certainly true, and part of God's design. But the family is so much more than that. God designed the family as a place in which we could begin to learn about His love. A small child can't really grasp the concept of an invisible Creator who loves her, but she can see Mommy's and Daddy's love, and later understand God's love because she's already experienced unconditional, accepting love.

We all know too that family doesn't always work the way it's supposed to. Some families are not even safe havens for the young of the species, much less a training ground for learning about unconditional love. Some families break apart. Some families abuse. Some families burden you with baggage you spend the rest of your life getting rid of so you can have whole, happy relationships.

Even the best families have weaknesses and shortcomings. None of us lives up to the ideal of perfectly reflecting God's love to our family members all the time.

You came from a family. You may have begun creating a family of your own. You've observed the families of your friends. You know that when family is good, it's very good. It's pretty much impossible to get a better start in life than you can get from a caring, loving family. And I hope you know too that when families fail, when they let you down, God is still there. He promised to be a father to the fatherless, and He's there for you when you need family.

When I asked people to share stories about family with me, I got good stories and bad stories (mostly good ones, though). In each, someone saw God through (or in spite of) the ups and downs of family life. I hope you'll see Him there too.

16.

YOU'RE UNIQUE

Fifteen-year-old Kim sat at the kitchen table, finishing homework. It was late. Her sister and brother had already gone to bed. The kitchen was lit by the single lamp hanging over the table—a cozy, intimate glow that flooded the sheets of loose-leaf paper.

Kim's mom finished putting away a few dishes in the cupboard and sat down across the table from her. "Homework finished?" she asked.

"Yeah, just about."

"What was the big assignment, anyway?"

"Oh, an essay for social studies class. About human rights around the world." Kim looked down at her books and papers spread out around her. "You know, I never realized all these things were going on in the world before I started researching this paper. Did you know there are still people being tortured in some parts of the world? And being put in jail for their religious beliefs? Or for speaking out against the government? That's not right, is it?"

"It certainly isn't."

"I know it's kind of a dumb thing to say, but I wish there was something I could do about it."

"That's not a dumb thing to say at all," Kim's mother said.

"But, you know, I'm just one person, one teenage girl. What difference can I make?"

Homework and housework both slipped into the background. Kim and her mom settled in for a long deep discussion. Their conversation ranged from human rights to individual responsibility, from religion to politics, from the far side of the world to the guy who sat next to Kim in math class.

Kim and her mom had always had a good relationship. She felt comfortable confiding in her mother. But this was the first time she had really shared with her mother—or anyone else—all the thoughts, questions, ideas, and dreams that crowded her mind. Kim needed to talk about the big issues—her fear that the world might end with a nuclear holocaust, her dreams of choosing a career that would allow her to make a difference in the world, her doubts about everything she'd been taught in church and Sabbath school. Things she lay awake at night thinking about but couldn't put into words.

So Kim talked. And her mom listened. Her mother asked questions, offered opinions, debated a few issues with her. But mostly Kim talked and her mother listened.

An hour slipped by, then another. Neither of them noticed the hands of the stove clock turning. Nobody suggested going to bed.

When Kim finally did look at the clock, she was shocked. She knew she was sleepy, but she'd never dreamed it could be almost 5:00 in the morning.

"Look out the window, Mom," she said. "It's almost dawn."

Kim's mother stood up, stretched, and looked out at the horizon. Sure enough, a faint glow of light told them they'd spent the entire night talking.

"I'm sorry," Kim said. "I made you miss a whole night's sleep just listening to me ramble on."

Her mom shook her head. "I don't mind a bit. I wouldn't want to do it every night, but it was worth it just to hear what's on your mind. You know, you're probably the only 15-year-old in the world who thinks about things like this."

Kim headed to her bedroom to catch a couple hours' sleep before getting up to go to school and turn in her social studies paper. All day she felt sleepy, but she also felt a warm glow that took more than a single day to fade. It wasn't that she and her mom had solved any of the world's great issues or that her mom had been able to give her easy answers to her troubling questions. It was just the special memory of an entire night with her mother's undivided attention, and those final words: "You're probably the only 15-year-old in the world who thinks about things like this." She was special. In her mother's eyes, she was absolutely unique.

Kim grew up. She became a high school teacher. And over many years of working with teenagers, she's learned a few things.

Kim discovered that she wasn't the only 15-year-old in the world who thought about those things. She's met many teenagers since who struggle with the same issues, the same concerns, the same big ideas she did at 15. She wasn't unique after all.

But someone else was. "Now that I work with teenagers," Kim says, "I know that the person who was unique was not me, but a mother who was willing to listen and marvel."

Not everyone is as fortunate as Kim was—not everyone has parents who are willing to listen, to pay real attention to you, to give you their undivided attention and celebrate your unique and special nature. If you have a parent like that, it's a blessing. When you have children of your own—or if you already do—you'll have the opportunity to show that same kind of interest and know what a gift it is.

Each of us has someone in our lives who needs us to listen. A child, a parent, a friend, a spouse, a brother or sister, coworker, or student. Someone needs you to sit down across the table and give them your undivided attention—maybe all night, if that's what it takes. Someone needs you to affirm that you are unique and special in their eyes.

**The purposes of a man's heart are deep waters,
but a man of understanding draws them out.
Proverbs 20:5, NIV.**

THINK IT THROUGH

1. Could a scene like this have happened in your home when you were growing up? Were you encouraged to talk about your thoughts and feelings?

2. When you pray, do you sense that God is really listening to you?

3. Whom can you think of who needs your listening ear right now?

17.

DANGLING IN MIDAIR

Peter grew up on a farm. One day when he was about 8 years old the whole family was at work baling hay. Peter was riding on the wagonful of hay, up the barn bridge into the barn. After a long hot day of hard work, Peter was looking for a little excitement when he noticed a steel pole above the barn door. He stood up, reached high, and grabbed the pole, yelling "Look at me!" to his sisters. His plan was to let go of the pole and drop back onto the wagon before it finished passing beneath him.

But Peter misjudged the timing, and suddenly he realized that the back of the wagon had slipped away beneath him. He was left dangling in midair, high above the ground, his feet kicking and his hands suddenly slippery. He had absolutely no desire to fall 10 feet or more to the ground.

Fortunately, one of his sisters saw his predicament and yelled, "Dad! Pete needs help!" Their father was driving the tractor pulling the wagon. When his daughter yelled, he stopped the tractor, jumped off, and ran to where Peter hung.

Peter felt a huge surge of relief when he saw his dad coming. Like most 8-year-olds, he had a lot of faith in his father's ability to handle a crisis situation. He didn't realize just how much of a crisis it was until he saw his father reaching up as high as he could. With his best efforts, Dad could just barely brush Peter's feet.

This didn't give Peter a lot of confidence. He was pretty sure

Dad wasn't going to be able to get much of a grip on his feet, and although his fingers were slipping and his arms getting tired, he didn't want to let go of the pole if his dad wasn't going to be able to catch him.

"Come on, son. Just let go. You'll drop a little, and I'll catch you," his father urged.

Peter wanted to, but he couldn't. He just didn't have enough faith. He pictured himself hurtling past his father and landing hard on the ground. How many bones would he break? How many did he have?

"Come on, Peter. I'll catch you," his dad repeated.

Finally Peter reached the point of desperation. He couldn't really hold on much longer. He trusted his dad to catch him—because he had no choice left. He let go of the pole. He dropped. He felt his dad's arms grab his waist. He was safe.

This is a true story, but there's a parable with much the same message, in which God tells a person clinging to a rope on the side of a mountain that He can save them only if they let go of the rope. It's a pretty good illustration of faith. So often in life we cling to the only security we have, even if it's dangerous and virtually useless. God's requirement—that we let go of our own sense of security in order to let Him catch us—sounds crazy. And so often we don't take that leap of faith till we really have no other choice—we have no strength left in our hands; we're letting go and falling anyway.

Can you imagine Peter's father walking away at that point, leaving his child to free-fall, then turning back to say, "Sorry, you didn't have enough faith. If you had, you would have let go of the pole sooner. Too bad you didn't choose to trust me when you still had a choice."

I can't imagine any father doing that, especially our heavenly Father. I don't have the greatest, strongest faith in the world, yet He accepts me, catches me in His arms, even when I've made Him my last resort. Because, you see, He loves me.

The eternal God is your refuge, and underneath are the everlasting arms. Deuteronomy 33:27, NIV.

Dangling in Midair

THINK IT THROUGH

1. Has someone in your family been there to "catch" you when you needed them? When and how?

2. Do you respond readily to God in faith, or do you trust Him only when you're desperate?

18.
LOW-FAT, LOW-CALORIE

Andrea was cooking for a big family dinner. Her dad and mom, her brother, and his wife were all invited. She wanted to make something festive for dessert, but her dad's recent heart trouble ruled out most of the high-calorie treats the family was used to.

She looked over her kitchen shelves, trying to decide what she had on hand that would make a tasty yet healthful dessert. She had a large bag of pecans on hand, and fleetingly thought how nice pecan pie would taste, but quickly rejected it as being far too decadent for her dad's restricted diet.

After another survey of her cupboards, she was back to the pecans. She flipped open her favorite all-purpose cookbook and looked at the pecan pie recipe. Just as she had suspected, it was anything but a "light" recipe. Three eggs! But maybe she could use one of those egg substitutes—weren't there some of those around somewhere? And light margarine could substitute for the butter . . .

Almost before she realized what she was doing, Andrea was making a pecan pie. But this was going to be a virtuous pecan pie. No evil ingredients; something her whole family, Dad included, could enjoy.

Of course, it would have to be cholesterol-free, so those eggs had to go. She rummaged around for the egg substitute and discovered she was nearly out. Throwing in the little she had, she decided to add some egg whites instead of whole eggs to the recipe.

Low-fat, Low-calorie

Next, the corn syrup—Andrea lifted the bottle and realized that it too was almost empty. But it was too late to turn back now—she'd already made a piecrust and sacrificed a number of innocent eggs.

Well, she figured, *syrup is basically sugar and water, so that's what I'll use—sugar and water.* Hadn't she read in a cookbook somewhere that you could do that? She wasn't sure how much it would take to equal a cup of syrup, but she took a guess.

When the mixture was spread in the pie plate and ready to go in the oven, it looked and smelled pretty much like every other pecan pie Andrea had ever made. She was pleased with her accomplishment. Low-fat, low-calorie cooking wasn't such a big deal.

Her regular pecan pie recipe said to bake it 40 to 50 minutes, or until the filling was set. Forty-five usually worked in Andrea's oven. But after 45 minutes this pie showed no sign of setting. Maybe those healthier ingredients just needed a little longer to come together.

Fifty minutes passed, then an hour. Andrea stuck a fork into the pie and found the filling as sticky and gooey as ever.

An hour and 15 minutes. Still no progress. Andrea left the kitchen and went upstairs to do a little tidying up. Almost everything else was ready for tonight's meal—maybe she should run out to a bakery to get something for dessert.

The smell drew her back downstairs. The unmistakable scorched-sugar smell of something burning in the oven.

Horrified, Andrea opened the oven door to discover that the pecan pie was a bubbling, boiling mass that had spilled out of its shell and onto the heating element. Flames licked up around the pie plate.

Slamming the oven door shut, she grabbed her box of baking soda, opened the door again, and flung the contents into the flames, praying it would work.

It did. The fire sputtered and died. Andrea looked sadly at the seething mass of pecan pie, one half now liberally covered with baking soda.

She took it out of the oven. She tried to scrape off the baking soda. Obviously the pie still hadn't set. And there didn't seem to be much point in leaving it in the oven any longer. She laid it on the counter and got busy with the rest of her dinner preparations.

CONNECTING

Things got busy, as they often do, and in the end there was no time to run to a bakery or even to make a batch of chocolate-chip cookies before the family arrived. Andrea pushed the thought of dessert to the back of her mind and sat her family down to the tasty meal she had so carefully prepared.

When dinner was over, before she began to clear the table, she started in on the little speech she'd prepared. "I'm really sorry there's no dessert tonight. I started to make a pecan pie, but . . . "

Andrea recited an abbreviated version of her tale of disaster. There was no need for her family to know about the fire or the baking soda: if she told them she'd tried to make a low-fat version of the pie and it hadn't set, that would be enough. She'd get credit for having tried, and extra credit for trying to accommodate her dad's diet. And nobody *really* needed dessert after such a big meal, anyway.

"Aw, that's too bad, honey. Did you throw it out?" her mom asked.

"Uh, no, I just left it on the kitchen counter," Andrea admitted.

"Well, you should go check on it. You know, it might have set up after it was left to sit a little."

"I sure do like pecan pie," her brother added.

"It doesn't have to be perfect, dear—we'll still enjoy it," her husband assured her.

"That was so nice of you, to try to make a pie just for me," her dad said.

Giddy with the compliments and approval of her family, Andrea made a fatal decision—the pecan pie deserved another chance. Maybe it had set after all.

There it sat on the kitchen counter, golden and gleaming. It certainly looked nice, now that it wasn't boiling like a witches' cauldron. Andrea pressed a tentative finger against the shining surface. To her amazement, it was firm. The pie had set!

She picked up a knife and tested again. Yes, it was firm. It was very firm. It had set and then some. She tried a little harder to push the knife in. It made no impact.

"Hey, gang, it's set, but I still don't know if it's . . . " Andrea called out, reaching up to a higher shelf for one of her sharper

Low-fat, Low-calorie

knives. At that moment she brushed against a large can of beans and knocked them off the shelf. The can fell two feet down to the counter, landed squarely in the middle of the pecan pie, bounced off, and rolled to a stop nearby. Andrea stared at the surface of the pie in amazement. The can had not even made a small dent in the impenetrable surface of her pecan pie.

Overcome by helpless giggles, Andrea submitted to her fate and carried the pie out to the dining room. "Oooh, it looks lovely," everyone chorused.

Andrea sat down, still unable to speak for laughter. Finally the whole story came out—the fire, the baking soda, the tin can, everything. After everyone had made a few tentative tries at the pie with their forks and knives, they were all laughing as hard as she was.

But they insisted she cut it—if she could. They all wanted to try it. With superhuman strength, Andrea managed to maneuver her sharpest knife through the heavy mass of pecan pie. It took a while to carve out a piece for everyone. That effort was followed by some slow, thoughtful chewing.

Once you got past the consistency, which was similar to that of Super-Glue or some other powerful adhesive, the actual taste of the pie wasn't bad. It was sweet, and you could taste the pecans. There was a lingering aura of baking soda, but only for those unlucky enough to eat from the wrong side of the pie.

Andrea looked around at her family in amazement. Every single one of them was actually eating the pecan pie. It wasn't going down easily, but it was going down. And amid their laughter, they were actually finding nice things to say about her disastrous dessert.

Unconditional love comes to us in lots of packages. Some people show their love by making heroic journeys or offering great sacrifices. Some give expensive gifts, and some forgive heinous sins. But for Andrea, a powerful image of her family's unconditional love is the picture of each of them doggedly chewing away at her pecan pie.

A friend loves at all times, and a brother is born for adversity. Proverbs 17:17, NIV.

THINK IT THROUGH

1. How have the people you care about shown unconditional love to you? How have you shown it to them?

2. In what ways have family members helped you to understand God's love?

19.

IN YOUR EYES

Steve was graduating from college. His mom was flying out for his graduation. He was a little nervous about her coming out, because she would be meeting his girlfriend, Claire, for the first time.

Steve had been dating Shelly for years. And years and years. They had started dating in junior high and dated on and off ever since. Maybe it was the "on and off" part that had made the relationship so painful in the end. He and Shelly had ended up hurting each other quite a lot, and it wasn't an easy relationship to recover from. She was part of his past, someone his family knew, someone who'd been in and out of his house since they were kids.

With Claire, Steve finally felt as if he'd left the past behind. He wasn't tied to Shelly and to those painful memories anymore. New beginnings stretched before him—and not just because of college graduation.

Still, he felt nervous about how his mom would react. For so many years his family had assumed he and Shelly would someday get married. His mom wasn't exactly disappointed that his relationship with Shelly had finally ended, but she had known Shelly, liked her, been used to her. Steve wondered how she'd take to Claire, who was so different in every way.

Steve drove two hours to the airport to pick up his mom on the Thursday before graduation weekend. They hugged each other, collected her luggage, and drove back to campus, catching up on all the news from home.

They were close to campus when Steve said, "Claire couldn't be here tonight, Mom, but she's really looking forward to meeting you. She's going to meet us for breakfast tomorrow, if that's OK."

"Of course I'm looking forward to meeting her," Steve's mom said. Then she added, "You know, I think she's the right girl for you."

"What?" Steve had hoped to hear those words, but not so soon—certainly not before his mother had even met Claire. "How can you say that? You've never even seen her."

"No, but I can see you. I know how unhappy you were a lot of that time you were with Shelly. And I can see how happy, how relaxed and content you are now. I can see it in your eyes—you've found something that's good for you. And that's what counts."

Steve had a lot of time to think about his mother's words, because, though he had no premonition of it at the time, his mother wasn't going to be with him much longer. She died unexpectedly not long after. She didn't live to see Steve and Claire marry and enjoy a happy, successful life together. She didn't live to see how right her assessment had been—Steve was, indeed, much happier and more at peace with Claire in his life.

This story says something about what a good relationship, a good marriage, should be. In a good relationship each of us should be better, happier, more fulfilled than we would otherwise be. I believe it's part of God's plan for marriage that we should grow further in the right relationship than we could do on our own.

That being said, I guess I could have put this story in the Love and Romance section, but I was struck, more than anything, by what it had to say about family—about the relationship between Steve and his mom. She knew him well enough to see in his eyes the difference between a happy and an unhappy relationship. She could hear it in his voice. She didn't even need to meet the girl—she knew her son, and she recognized when he was happy.

We need people like that in our lives. If we're blessed with a strong biological family, we need those people—our parents and siblings—to know us, to understand what we're feeling, to recognize warning signs and signs that something good is happening. If we don't have that kind of relationship with our blood family, we need to build a network of friends who do know us that well.

Family members, especially parents, get a bad reputation when it comes to judging relationships. How many times have you heard someone say, "My parents just don't understand . . . they think my boyfriend's all wrong for me . . . but they just don't know him like I do!"

Granted, parents have been wrong about these things. (Look at Romeo and Juliet.) But they have also been right—especially when they know you well enough to recognize what makes you happy or unhappy. That may not make it any easier to accept the advice of a friend or family member who thinks the one you love is all wrong for you—but perhaps that person's opinion will carry more weight if she's spent years looking into your eyes, knowing you better than anyone else.

> **May your fountain be blessed,**
> **and may you rejoice in the wife of your youth.**
> **Proverbs 5:18, NIV.**

THINK IT THROUGH

1. If you're married or in a serious dating relationship now, can you honestly say you "rejoice" in that relationship? Can your family and friends see that you are happy?

2. Who in your life knows you well enough to recognize when you are happy or unhappy? Does that person give his or her opinion honestly? Do you accept it when they do?

20.

GRANDMA KNOWS BEST

A trip to Grandma's house is a treat for most children. It wasn't that way for Dee-anne and her brothers. Several times a year their parents took them to visit Grandma, but it was never an occasion to look forward to.

Grandma didn't have a child-friendly house. Her large home—which would have been excellent for playing hide-and-seek or exploring, under different circumstances—was flawlessly decorated and filled with breakable knickknacks. The phrases "Don't touch," "Don't get that dirty," and "Stay away from that" rang through the air constantly whenever the children were at Grandma's house.

In fact, Grandma herself wasn't really a child-friendly person. She didn't like to tell stories or play dress-up. She liked to dress up, herself, for parties and visits. She liked to show off her house when her acquaintances came to visit. If her grandchildren were present at the time, she liked them to make an appearance, clean, well dressed, and silent—then go away. If one of them had earned good grades in school or won an award, Grandma would tell her friends about it. She liked prizes and awards.

As Dee-anne grew up she understood that her grandmother was most impressed by external things. Dee-anne's dad worked as an auto mechanic, while her uncle was a dentist. Grandma didn't make any secret of the fact that she thought one of her sons had done much better than the other. Whenever Dee-anne's dad was around,

Grandma Knows Best

Grandma made pointed remarks about "how well your brother is doing with his career—what a successful man he is." Once, in front of the whole family, she came out and said, "I don't know why you turned out to be such a failure."

Dee-anne was angry at Grandma for hurting her dad. But as she herself grew older she became a favorite of Grandma's. Dee-anne excelled in school and won several scholarships. Grandma began to brag about Dee-anne. "That girl's going to be a success, mark my words," Grandma said.

Grandma was full of advice. "Make sure you get into a good university," she told Dee-anne. "Choose your classes wisely—you don't want to waste your time." When she heard Dee-anne had made the dean's list in her first year, Grandma wrote a proud letter of congratulations. Dee-anne enjoyed the letter—until she came to the part in which Grandma said, "I'm so pleased someone in your family is making something of themselves—your brothers are such a disappointment."

She just can't stop criticizing and comparing, Dee-anne thought.

Grandma admired people who made a lot of money, who had nice houses, who had impressive careers. With Dee-anne's good grades in social studies and her gift for public speaking, Grandma had encouraged her to study law, and for her first two years in college Dee-anne was a prelaw major.

The problem was, she hated it. She was getting good grades, but it just wasn't interesting. What she really liked was visual art—painting had always been her hobby, and now she began taking art classes whenever she could fit them into her schedule. By the end of her second year Dee-anne had to admit, to herself and to everyone else, that she wasn't going to be a lawyer. She switched her major to fine arts.

Most of her friends and family were supportive. Grandma was furious. "No granddaughter of mine is going to university to learn to paint pictures! And exactly how do you expect to support yourself?"

Dee-anne wasn't quite sure. Today, with college long behind her, she still isn't exactly sure how she supports herself. She sells a few paintings every year, does some commercial art, teaches some art classes. She isn't rich—some years she barely makes middle class. But she loves her work. She feels fulfilled and looks forward to getting out of bed every morning.

Grandma is older now, but she hasn't mellowed. Her comments about Dee-anne's career are still sharp and cutting. She isn't impressed when Dee-anne has a show in a local gallery or when her artwork appears on a magazine cover—Dee-anne's success doesn't count.

Dee-anne still finds herself clipping reviews of her shows to send to Grandma, trying to win her approval. Sometimes she feels her grandmother looking over her shoulder. Once she sold a painting and was angry at herself for days because she hadn't asked a higher price for it. When she finally asked herself, *Why does the money matter to me? I don't particularly need it right now,* she realized what the answer was—Grandma. Grandma placed more value on things that cost more.

Sometimes Dee-anne looks around the comfortable house she decorated herself and thinks, *It's just not good enough.* The image before her mind's eye is of Grandma's professionally decorated, untouched showplace.

Dee-anne managed to break free of her grandmother's expectations for her life and do the things she really wanted to do. But she's found it hard to shake that inner voice that tells her she has to live up to Grandma's standards. She sometimes finds it difficult to ignore the question "What would Grandma think about this?"

But she's learning. Learning to apply what she's known for years—that Grandma didn't really know best. Grandma's standards are not Dee-Anne's standards—nor are they God's standards. Slowly Dee-Anne is learning she doesn't have to live up to anyone's expectations but her own and God's.

Let us stop passing judgment on one another. Instead, make up your mind not to put any stumbling block or obstacle in your brother's way. Romans 14:13, NIV.

THINK IT THROUGH

1. Have you ever had to deal with an important person in your life who exhibited a critical, judgmental spirit? Have you been able to separate yourself from this person's criticism?

2. If we are required to live life only by God's standards, not by those of other people, how are we to determine for ourselves what God's expectations for us are?

21.

"AREN'T YOU BOB'S BOY?"

Sabbath morning, far from home. Really far, in fact, for two Midwestern kids. Debbie and Rick were visiting Hong Kong. Recently married, they were taking the trip of a lifetime, which was how they found themselves in Hong Kong on Sabbath.

They didn't know anyone. Hong Kong was a stopover, a tourist opportunity: they had no friends to visit and no acquaintances to look up. But they found the Seventh-day Adventist church, and they made it in time for Sabbath school.

Most things around them were unfamiliar—the faces, the voices, the songs, the service. There were hints of familiar sights and sounds, but even those seemed just slightly different, like objects seen through an out-of-focus lens. Maybe it was just exhaustion and jet lag, but Debbie and Rick felt out of place and off balance. They were the kind of Adventists who always looked for a local church to attend when they traveled—they were used to feeling like part of a worldwide family. Yet on the Sabbath morning in Hong Kong, farther from home than they'd ever been, they definitely didn't feel like they belonged.

Then, between Sabbath school and church, people began coming up to welcome them. It was a friendly church. Members went out of their way to meet the visitors and see that they were comfortable.

Inevitably, this small Adventist world being what it is, Debbie and Rick had to explain where they'd come from. What Adventist college they'd attended in the U.S., where Rick had spent a year as a student missionary, where their home towns were. Who in Hong Kong would know the names of the small towns in Wisconsin and Indiana that they called home?

Suddenly one man broke into a broad smile. Grabbing Rick's hand, he said, "Aren't you Bob Davidson's boy? I knew your father when I was in the U.S.—we went to Andrews University together!"

Rick started to grin. "That's my dad! What years were you there? Did you ever meet my mom?" All around, people laughed and shook their heads. A small, small world.

In one moment, with one link forged, Debbie and Rick were no longer among strangers, but among friends. They had something in common. They also had an invitation home to Sabbath dinner.

As we have opportunity, let us do good to all people, especially to those who belong to the family of believers. Galatians 6:10, NIV.

THINK IT THROUGH

1. Have you ever experienced the sense of being part of a world-wide "family" of believers, even when far from home? If so, when and where?

2. Why does the concept of the church as a family sometimes fail? Have you experienced this?

3. What's one specific thing you can do this week to make your church more like a family, and to welcome others into that family?

22.

MY FATHER'S NAME

In the summer of 1954, when he was 17 years old, my father fell in love.

Not with my mother (that came later).

The object of his affection was a Gibson Les Paul electric guitar in Hutton's Music Store. It cost $295; the amplifier was an additional $150. It sounds like a steal in today's money, but you have to remember that this was 1954 and my father was earning $30 a week working at his dad's printshop.

A couple weeks passed with my dad stopping by the music store day after day, gazing at the guitar, trying to get up the nerve to talk to Mr. Hutton. Finally he proposed a deal. He had an old guitar he could trade in for $75, and he could scrape together $25 cash. That left $345. This was long before the era of credit cards—if my dad wanted credit, Mr. Hutton would have to trust him.

Mr. Hutton did. He agreed to let my dad take the guitar with $100 down and pay off the remainder at $5 a week. Week after week for the next year my dad went to Hutton's and passed over $5. Meanwhile, he delighted in playing his beautiful new instrument.

The following autumn my dad left home to join the Air Force. Before leaving, he went to Hutton's Music Store one last time. He brought with him the balance owed on the guitar—about $25 or $30—and thanked Mr. Hutton for trusting him to pay off such a large sum of money over such a short period of time. After all, not every store owner would have been willing to trust a teenager with such a large debt.

Mr. Hutton's reply surprised my dad. "I never worried about the money," he said. "You're Mac Morgan's son."

Recounting the incident years later, my dad said, "I had unknowingly been trading on my father's reputation." His printer father was a businessman with a reputation for honest dealing in the community, and his son benefited from that reputation for honesty.

Now, almost a half century later, the Les Paul guitar still has an honored place in my father's house—and my son, when he was still barely able to talk, would burst into the house and ask, "Grampa play his Gibson Les Paul guitar?" And I still have such respect for my father's and grandfather's name that I kept it as part of my own even after I married and added my husband's name—because of what the name Morgan stands for.

I guess the parallel is obvious. We Christians all bear the family name of God our Father, Christ our Elder Brother. And we trade on that name's reputation. Because we call God our Father, people expect certain things from us. Honesty. Justice. Kindness. Love.

Unlike my dad in his dealings with Mr. Hutton, we Christians don't always live up to everything our Father's name represents. And yes, He forgives. Yes, He is full of mercy, grace, and compassion. But that doesn't change the fact that when we mess up we drag His name through the dirt. We change—maybe forever—someone's image of what a Christian is, what our God stands for.

It's a heavy responsibility, bearing our Father's name. It's a fantastic gift, too. Even more valuable than a 1953 Gibson Les Paul.

**You shall not take the name of the
Lord your God in vain, for the Lord
will not hold him guiltless who takes
His name in vain. Exodus 20:7, NKJV.**

**Some trust in chariots and some in horses,
but we trust in the name of the
Lord our God. Psalm 20:7, NIV.**

CONNECTING

THINK IT THROUGH

1. How do you respond to the idea that everything you do reflects on God's reputation?

2. Why does the Bible place so much emphasis on the "name" of God, on praying in the "name" of Jesus? What power does a name have?

23.

SACRIFICE

It wasn't originally my intention to end this section on family with two stories about electric guitars. I had the story about my dad's Les Paul in here, and I liked the point it made, and I was going to leave that as the final story in this section. But then my friend Adam told me another story about an electric guitar that I wanted to share too.

When Adam was 13 he got interested in learning to play the guitar. He really, really wanted his own electric guitar. He hung out at music stores and looked at ads in the paper. He looked long enough to know that he didn't have the faintest hope of getting a good guitar anytime soon.

Adam's parents were divorced, and he lived with his mom. Her income as a single parent didn't stretch to include electric guitars. It was already stretched enough trying to cover such things as groceries, rent, heat, and light. Adam had spent enough time hearing his mom complain about her tight budget and how short funds were that he knew there wasn't much point asking for a guitar.

As Christmas drew near he dropped a couple hints about how great it would be if he had his own guitar. Maybe his mom would be able to give him some money, and then if he could manage to do some odd jobs and save for a while, in a few months he'd be able to get some kind of secondhand guitar or something. It wasn't what he really wanted, but at 13 Adam was already old enough to understand the difference between dreams and reality.

CONNECTING

Christmas morning came. Adam decided he was too old that year to race out to the tree before dawn and get all excited about shaking and squeezing packages. He was just going to lie in bed and play it cool. He managed to do that till about 7:00 a.m., but then he just had to get up and go see what was under that tree.

He was surprised to find that his mom was already up. She looked more eager to open the presents than he was. Adam didn't know why. It wasn't as though he'd been able to get her anything really great— just some perfume from the drugstore. But she looked excited.

"Come on, Adam; don't you want to open your presents?" she urged.

That was when he knew something was up. And then he spotted the package—the long narrow package under the tree, just about the size of, well, an electric guitar.

Adam's heart leaped up in his throat. He had—he was almost 100 percent certain he had—a guitar! As he dove for the package and began to tear at the wrapping, he was already telling himself to calm down. Any guitar Mom could afford couldn't be a very expensive or classy guitar. Maybe it was secondhand. He'd have to remember not to be disappointed. He just had to focus on how cool it was to have a guitar at all.

Then the last bit of wrapping was gone, the case was opened, and Adam looked at his brand new Fender Stratocaster.

(For those of you who aren't guitar-wise, this is kind of like the Gibson Les Paul in the last story: this is a Very Nice Guitar. Also pretty pricey.)

Adam was speechless. He knew how much a Fender Strat cost, because he'd been staring at them in the stores for months. He cradled the beautiful instrument reverently in his hands. It was a full minute before he remembered to say, "Thanks, Mom." He said it in a hushed voice, kind of like a prayer.

To this day Adam, now a college student, still doesn't know exactly how his mom paid for that guitar. But he knows it took sacrifice. She had to give up something—probably quite a lot of things—in order to fulfill that dream for him. Not to put food on the table or clothes on his back, but to give him a luxury, something he didn't need but desperately wanted.

Adam would have been happy with any relatively decent guitar. But his mom went above and beyond. She sacrificed to give him the very best—something far beyond what he'd ever have dared to ask for.

Family love, at its best, is supposed to be a reflection of God's love. God put us in families so He could show His love to us in a tangible way, through each other. This doesn't always work out. In Adam's family it already hadn't worked out perfectly. There had been divorce, division, disunity. But God was still at work. Through his mother's love Adam caught a glimpse of a kind of love that is sacrificial, generous, prodigal. A love that gives far more than is expected, at tremendous cost. A love, in fact, just like God's love.

Adam didn't appreciate that right away. At the time, all he knew was that he had an awesome guitar and an awesome mom. But looking back, he clearly sees the reflection of an awesome gift-giving God in that Christmas morning years ago—which is what we're all supposed to see, when we look back at Christmas morning.

**Now to him who is able to do immeasurably more than all we ask or imagine, according to his power that is at work within us, to him be glory in the church and in Christ Jesus throughout all generations, for ever and ever! Amen.
Ephesians 3:20, 21, NIV.**

THINK IT THROUGH

1. What's the most sacrificial thing any family member has ever done for you?

2. Have you ever given anyone a gift that involved real sacrifice?

3. Have you ever been surprised by God's grace—by how generously He gives? If so, when?

CHILDREN

Jesus recognized children as being a little bit special. Think of the things He had to say about them: "Unless you change and become like little children, you will never enter the kingdom of heaven"; "Let the little children come to me, and do not hinder them, for the kingdom of heaven belongs to such as these"; "Whoever welcomes one of these little children in my name welcomes me" (Matthew 18:3; Matthew 19:14; Mark 9:37, NIV). Jesus was, as we say about people sometimes, "good with children."

I was never good with children. Don't get me wrong—I was never deliberately *bad* with children. But growing up as an only child, I had neither younger siblings nor nieces and nephews to get me used to little children. I didn't baby-sit much as a teenager. I didn't actively dislike babies and small children, but I didn't go out of my way to be with them either. Anytime I was left in the company of a small child, I felt somewhat awkward, especially if other adults were looking at me. I figured everyone was thinking, *What's wrong with her? Doesn't she know what to do with a child?* When I started teaching I jumped into high school teaching wholeheartedly (I've always liked teenagers since I stopped being one) and was always grateful God hadn't put me in elementary teaching.

All this changed, obviously, when I had my own children. In fact, within seconds of my first child's birth it changed so totally I could never have imagined feeling distant or ambivalent toward a baby. My feeling toward my own two kids was, and is, a total, all-consuming love affair that shows no sign of ever cooling down.

It was also a fantastic learning experience. Nothing quite beats the feeling you get when you hold your child in your arms and think about the many times in the Bible that God compares us to His children, and Himself to our father or mother. God loves us like a parent loves a child—it's a familiar formula, but the first time I looked at my baby in my arms and thought, *God loves me this much,* it blew my mind. I had not imagined that love so total, so selfless, so unconditional, could exist in my human heart. To realize that this was only a pale reflection of God's love for me was incredible.

I'm still amazed, day by day, at the lessons my children teach me. So are lots of other people—not just parents, but teachers, grandparents, anyone who gets down on a child's level and gets involved with them. I'll freely admit that in the stories that follow I'm totally shameless in talking about my own two children and what they've taught me. Maybe you'll see a little of God in these pages too.

24.

"HOLD ME; DON'T TOUCH ME!"

When my son was 2 years old he sometimes woke up cranky.

Not in the morning, though—oh no, at 6:30 a.m. he was the happiest, brightest, liveliest person you'd ever hope to meet. Actually, my fondest hope is never to have to meet *anyone* at 6:30 a.m., since I'm not a morning person by any stretch of the imagination. Christopher has always had a different agenda for mornings, one that involves being awake and having fun.

But later in the day, when he woke from his afternoon nap— that was a different story. Most days he would wake up crying bitterly, and for a half hour after the nap nothing pleased him.

"Wanna go downstairs?"

"Noooo! Wanna stay upstairs! I want something to *eeaat! . . . . Noooo!* I don't wanna eat that!"

You get the picture. In fact, if you've ever cared for a 2-year-old, you could probably draw and color the picture.

The only conceivable bright side to this habit was that sometimes Christopher would say, "Want to be in your arms! Want to be in your *arms!*" This wasn't so great if I was nursing his baby sister at the time, but otherwise it was a nice thing, because normally he was too much of a bundle of energy to want to cuddle. So if he'd actually get up in my arms and whimper and snivel through his cranky time, I'd get a little bit of cuddling in, and we'd both enjoy it.

Now, you sacrifice many things when you become a parent, and privacy is one of the biggest. In fact, the biggest dividing line between parents and nonparents is the basic life assumption that going to the bathroom is something you do all by yourself.

Before I had kids I never questioned this. It seemed obvious that you wouldn't have anyone else along for this most private of activities. But as soon as Christopher was born, things changed. Sometimes I could lay him in his crib and snatch a few seconds in the bathroom, but he was a fairly fussy baby, and often he just had to be with me. I learned I could go to the washroom while holding a squirming baby if I absolutely had to.

Things got even less private when he learned to crawl, then to walk. I couldn't shut the door and go to the bathroom, since that would mean leaving my curious toddler unsupervised. And once that door was open, why would he want to play all by himself in the hall? Of course he just toddled into the washroom. Later, when we began toilet-training him, I'd put him on his little potty whenever I had to use the big one, and we treated it as a team activity.

So I don't have a lot of concerns left about bathroom privacy. But on one particular day I thought Christopher might just have stepped over the line.

Naptime was over and crankytime was in full swing. Baby Emma was mercifully asleep, but Christopher was whining about anything and everything. After about 20 minutes of futile efforts to calm him down, I just had to go to the washroom. So I went in (sorry if this is getting a little too personal, but as I said, I have no sense of privacy anymore) and sat down.

Chris, of course, followed me in. "Want to be in your *arms,* Mommy!"

"In a minute, Chris, when I get finished in the bathroom."

"No! *No! No!* Want to be in your arms *now!*" The "now" turned into one of these eerie blood-curdling howls that issue from the throats of wild dogs. My son is a man of action as well as words. Still howling, he came over and began to crawl up on my lap.

"Hold Me; Don't Touch Me!"

Now, this is not a situation I would have ever imagined in my preparent days. I'm on the toilet, answering the call of nature, and a sweaty, crying 2-year-old is sitting on my lap, facing in toward me with his head on my chest and his legs wrapped around me.

For one split second I considered trying to pry him off and put him on the floor. But something more than the fear of his shrieks stopped me. At moments like these I'm always vividly reminded of how short his babyhood is going to be. Very soon—before these words are even published between the covers of a book—he will be big, tough, independent, and gearing up for kindergarten. He won't need Mommy. And I will yearn for him to need me that much again.

So I savor moments like these instead of rejecting them. I put my arms around him and held him close, marveling at how my personal space was suddenly the least important thing in my world.

Then something funny happened. I began rubbing my hands along Christopher's bare arms, enjoying the silky smooth feel of his baby skin and humming a little tune to him. Despite the odd location, I was really enjoying this mother-son moment.

But he began pulling his arms away, grabbing at my hands, pushing my fingers away from his arms. Though he still remained latched onto me like a magnet, he squirmed away from the touch of my hands. (As I said, at moments like this *nothing* pleases him.) "No, Mommy, don't touch me. Don't touch me," he whimpered.

Despite his protests I hugged him tighter, stifling a laugh. The irony of the moment hit me hard. Here is a tiny individual so completely dependent on me, so much in need of me, that he will come and sit on my lap while I go to the bathroom—yet he's still defiantly waving his little flag of independence, pretending he doesn't need me to soothe or comfort him. He wants loving, but it has to be on his terms.

And that got me thinking, as my children always do, about me and God. I understand the analogy of God as a parent so much better now, in so many more ways, than I ever did before I had children. This moment was one of those when I couldn't help thinking, *Do I do this to God?*

"Hold me, but don't touch me," I tell my heavenly Father. I

need Him desperately, and I recognize that need instinctively, running to Him for comfort when life comes down on me too hard. Yet when I feel His touch my independence asserts itself, and I squirm away. "Don't touch me! Don't get too involved in my life! Don't try to change me!"

Hold me; don't touch me. We tell Him that all the time as our human need for control vies with our need for Him. Shelter me, protect me from evil, solve my problems, and answer my prayers—but don't get too close. Don't reach those strong hands of Yours too far into my life. I need You, Lord, but only on my own terms.

A child journeys into greater and greater independence, farther away from those sheltering arms that once supplied his every need. But our journey of faith has to be in the opposite direction—closer and closer to Father, farther and farther away from our own self-reliance.

Lord, let the day come soon when I will let You hold me *and* touch me—when I will not squirm away from Your gentle hands.

And also, Lord, give me a few more good cuddles with Christopher before he's too big to need me.

**The eternal God is your refuge,
and underneath are the everlasting arms.
Deuteronomy 33:27, NIV.**

THINK IT THROUGH

1. When have you felt most in need of God to "hold" you?

2. Do you think you are becoming more or less dependent on God?

3. Are there any areas of your life that you are not allowing God to touch? What would it mean to let Him "touch" you?

25.

IN THE FULLNESS OF TIME

as anybody called my doctor yet?"

The nurse looked at me with what I assume was supposed to be a patient smile, and rolled her eyes. "We called and told him that you'd come in, and he said that he had a few more patients to see and that he'd be over right after that."

"So when can I get moved to the birthing room?"

"Just as soon as we're convinced that you're really in labor."

"What do I have to do to convince you of that?"

The nurse chuckled, shuffling some papers on her desk. "Oh, some moaning and groaning would help."

I don't know if any other expectant mothers have ever had this problem, but here I was on the labor and delivery floor of my local hospital, having labor pains, completely unable to convince the nursing staff that I was actually going to have a baby. The fact that I wasn't writhing and screaming in agony, combined with the fact that the readings on their little labor monitor machine apparently weren't impressive enough for them, caused these nice women to shake their heads knowingly at each other. I could imagine them whispering among themselves, "Oh, another hysterical woman imagining she's in labor. Why, she's not due for another week yet. She doesn't even know what *real* labor pains feel like, or she wouldn't be in here wasting our time."

Now, if this had been my first baby, there might have been some justification for this. But in fact it was my second, and I had a pretty good idea of what labor pains felt like. They felt, at first, much like what I was currently experiencing. Then they escalated quickly—in my case, very quickly—into something resembling the feeling of having an ATV drive over your stomach. Repeatedly.

I know there are women who take hours and hours, even days, to produce a baby, but my first experience had made it pretty clear that I was not one of those. The whole process had taken me about nine hours, which everyone had told me was pretty quick for a first baby. Everyone had also told me that second babies come more quickly than the first—sometimes a lot more quickly.

My doctor had barely gotten there in time for the first baby to arrive: When I told him he was going to the hospital, he went home and went to bed, figuring he'd enjoy a night's sleep while I suffered agonizing pain. His plan, I guess, was to wake up bright and cheery and refreshed in the morning and show up in time for my delivery. Unfortunately for him, but fortunately for me, he had barely shut his eyes when the nurses called to say the baby was arriving any minute and would he please get up there as quickly as possible.

That was the first time. So as I went for my last prenatal visit with baby number 2, I warned the doctor, "Remember, when I go into labor, I go fast. So don't go home and take a nap this time!"

Obviously he hadn't heeded my warning. Here I was in the hospital, and, at least as far as I was concerned, I was well into the early stages of labor (even if the nurses didn't believe me). And what was his plan? See a few more patients, then pop over to the hospital to see how I was doing.

I didn't like this one bit.

Within the next few minutes the nurses changed their minds. Quickly. I went from being able to stroll down to the nurses' station and chat with them to lying doubled over on a bed unable to speak during contractions. Apparently there was now enough moaning and groaning to satisfy them.

In the Fullness of Time

"Even if your doctor doesn't get here in time," one said, "you don't need to worry. There are plenty of interns and residents around; there'll be someone to help you."

They said this as though it was good news, but I wasn't so sure. I mean, I was glad to hear about all the interns and residents, but it worried me that now even the nurses seemed to think my doctor might not make the 15-minute trip across town in time.

Just at this point an intern appeared. You may or may not remember an eighties TV show called *Doogie Howser, M.D.,* in which a brilliant child prodigy went to medical school at the age of like 15 or something and was practicing as a doctor before he was out of his teens. Anyway, when the intern showed up it was all I could do not to say (through my gritted teeth), "Hello, Doogie!"

This is something that happens when you get past 30—doctors start to look frighteningly young. This fresh-faced boy did not look capable of dealing with something as complicated as a birth.

But he introduced himself and assured me that he would be there to help in case my doctor didn't show up, and I said, "Good, because I think this baby is coming pretty quickly. My first one did, and this labor is moving even faster."

At that point another contraction hit, I was unable to see clearly for a while, and when I looked around again Doogie was gone.

Shortly after this I got moved to the nice birthing room. Unfortunately I was no longer in a position to appreciate the beauty of my surroundings. The nurses began to prepare themselves for some major event.

I won't get graphic from this point on . . . let's just say that the word "Push!" was repeated several times, and a very short time later a small red squalling bundle was deposited in my arms with the words "Mrs. Cole, you have a beautiful baby girl."

As I snuggled close to my precious Emma and made her acquaintance, a familiar voice said, "So, what's going on here?"

It was my doctor. He had missed the whole thing. The nurses had delivered Emma, and had done a fantastic job. A few minutes later in strolled Dr. Doogie Howser, who said, "Wow—when you said this was going to happen quickly, I should have believed you!"

CONNECTING

Well, yes, you should have. You all should have. Fortunately this story has a happy ending—an ecstatically happy ending, since it ends with me getting my beautiful, healthy, perfect daughter. I can't even stand to think about how it might have ended if the birth had been hampered by some complication that the nurses couldn't deal with. As it stands, it's a funny story for me to share with Emma someday; had circumstances been different, it could have been the beginning of a lifetime of anger, bitterness, and lawsuits, all aimed at a medical staff who wouldn't believe me when I said I was having a baby.

At the time I wasn't thinking of parables and allegories, but a little later it struck me how much the whole incident reminded me of being a Seventh-day Adventist, going around telling people that Jesus is coming again.

Usually, when I do mention it to people, they don't believe me. It doesn't seem possible. Things don't look as if the world is going to end. There's not much outward evidence that Jesus is coming again. No matter how much I warn people and tell them to be ready, they'll believe the evidence of their own eyes rather than listening to me. They find it easier to conclude that I just don't know what I'm talking about. Sometimes they almost convince me that they're right and I'm wrong. But someday Jesus, just like Emma, is going to make a sudden appearance that will shock everyone—and some people won't be ready.

Of course, there are a few flaws with this analogy. I *don't* tell people about Jesus' coming with the same urgency that I told the nurses I was in labor—because I'm not driven by that same inner certainty. And Jesus has been delaying His return a lot longer than four hours—which is how long my entire labor took. We could hold out against the world's cynicism and our own doubts for four hours. But for 2,000 years?

It's probably fair to point out here, as any woman who has given birth will know, that four hours of labor feels pretty much like 2,000 years while you're going through it. Time is meaningless in which you're in pain. It's meaningless to God, too, we're told, because He lives in an eternity where our millennium is His afternoon. All that matters is the outcome—as surely as a laboring woman will someday produce a baby, God will someday, certainly, bring an end to this earth's agony and begin something entirely fresh and new.

I wish I knew how to tell people—how to help them get ready. But as you've seen, convincing people that the situation is urgent isn't exactly my strong point. I hope they won't have to walk in, like my doctor, when it's all over and find they've missed the main event.

We know that the whole creation has been groaning as in the pains of childbirth right up to the present time. Not only so, but we ourselves, who have the firstfruits of the Spirit, groan inwardly as we wait eagerly for our adoption as sons, the redemption of our bodies. For in this hope we were saved. Romans 8:22-24, NIV.

While people are saying, "Peace and safety," destruction will come on them suddenly, as labor pains on a pregnant woman, and they will not escape. 1 Thessalonians 5:3, NIV.

THINK IT THROUGH

1. How urgent do you feel about Christ's second coming? If you do have a feeling of urgency, how are you able to communicate that to others?

2. Is it really realistic to still believe, 2,000 years after Christ's first advent, that He is coming again? What strengthens your faith in His return?

26.

"PRAY, MOMMY!"

Church seemed longer than usual that morning. Of course, church often seems long to the parents of a toddler. Sandra and Sam sat in their back-row pew, armed with an array of Cheerios, crayons, board books, stuffed toys, and sippy cups—everything it took to get Brandon through a one-hour church service.

Sandra was tired. She was five months pregnant and starting to feel it. Brandon had awakened three times the night before and had needed to be put back to bed, storied, and sung to sleep. This morning he was none the worse—he had his usual fund of unstoppable 18-month-old energy—but Sandra felt dragged out. Cradle roll Sabbath school had been one endless struggle to keep Brandon in his seat, and now she was trying to keep him quiet for church. The singing going on all around her didn't inspire her or uplift her spirit. She just wanted to crawl back into bed.

Stifling a yawn, Sandra flipped through the bulletin. Pastor Lake was preaching today—sometimes he went long. Sandra didn't think she could stand it if the service went past 12:00. It was just too long to try and keep Brandon occupied. Sometimes Brandon would crawl up on Sam's lap and fall asleep during the sermon. Maybe today would be one of those lucky days.

Song service ended; the praise team sat down; Elder Phillips stood up to give the welcome. All around, church members turned to shake hands and welcome each other and the visitors. Today

"Pray, Mommy!"

Sandra didn't get up to greet any visitors. She stayed in her pew and let people come to her with smiles and warm handshakes. Mostly they just wanted to talk to Brandon and say how cute he was, which was fine by her.

Then "Now, Dear Lord, as We Pray" began again, the signal for the whole congregation to slip to their knees. Today Sandra just didn't want to kneel. She was too tired, too stiff, too achy. Sam knelt down, and Sandra thought, *Good. He can have the job of setting a good example for Brandon today. I'm just going to sit here.*

In her heart she knew there was more going on than just a sore back and creaky knees. Something in her spirit didn't want to kneel before God today. She didn't want to go out and embezzle church funds or table-dance at men's clubs—she just wanted to rebel in a tiny private way. Just to say, *God, I'm not totally Yours. Today I want to belong to myself, to have things my way, to pity myself. Today I don't have the spunk or stamina to march in Your army—I just want to sit in my pew and sulk for a few minutes.*

Brandon sat on the pew beside her, chewing Cheerios. "It's time to pray, Brandon," Sam whispered. He gave Sandra an understanding smile, no doubt knowing that she didn't feel up to kneeling.

But Brandon wasn't so understanding. He hopped off the pew and knelt down beside his dad, folding his hands just the way he'd been taught. Then, as the strains of "Now, Dear Lord" faded away, he patted the floor beside him and said, "Pray, Mommy!"

Of course, it was the one request Sandra couldn't resist. God might have called her in the whirlwind or the earthquake, but in the still small voice of her 18-month-old son He had the surest way to get her attention. Sandra knelt beside Brandon, folded her hands, and closed her eyes, just as they taught in cradle roll. And miraculously, when her body assumed the position of surrender, so did her spirit. Weariness, self-pity, and rebellion slipped away, and she found, as she always did, that giving herself up to God was not work but rest. His arms were outstretched to hold her just as Sam's were to hold Brandon, and all through the church service both Sandra and her son rested in their Father's arms.

CONNECTING

The Lord is near to those who have a broken heart, and saves such as have a contrite spirit. Psalm 34:18, NKJV.

THINK IT THROUGH

1. Why do we traditionally kneel when we approach God? Is the posture of our bodies in prayer really important? How can our physical position help or hinder our prayers?

2. Why are we so often most rebellious against God at the times when we need Him most?

27.

MORE LIKE MYSELF

Both my children were born perfect.

I realize I may be in a little theological trouble here, since we have this doctrine of original sin to deal with, and apparently every human being is born with a natural bent toward evil. OK, I'll accept that on a doctrinal level, but I'm sure every mother and father on earth would agree with me that there is absolutely no evidence of evil apparent in a sweet, sleepy-eyed, soft-skinned newborn baby.

In every baby I've ever known, but particularly my own two, this state of absolute sinlessness continued for several months. (No, colic is not a sin. The baby can't help it. Repeat this slowly and carefully to yourself if you have a colicky baby in the house—or anywhere on your block—at the moment.) Yes, small babies can do things that are inconvenient or annoying, mostly having to do with crying, filling their diapers, and (not) sleeping—but these things are not done with any malicious forethought, any attempt to harm. The baby is simply being a baby.

From my limited observation as a parent, a baby's personality begins to unfold quite a while before any possibility of sin or evil appears. By the time my son, Christopher, was 6 months old we had a strong sense of who Christopher was. He loved to smile, he loved to laugh and make other people laugh. He responded strongly to music. He loved people; if I had him in the cart in a grocery store lineup and I was too busy loading my groceries onto the counter to talk to him, I would look down to find him playing peekaboo with the person in line behind me, or staring at an oblivious stranger as if to say, "Look at me! I'm cute! Don't you want to play with me?" He was a happy baby, a people person, a fun little guy.

I guess I'd have to say the possibility of "sinfulness" in a child doesn't develop until the ability to understand "No"—sometime shortly before the first birthday. Once babies can recognize that you want them to obey and can choose not to, I guess we have the very faint beginnings of that natural bent toward evil. My daughter, Emma (also a sunny, smiley, beautiful baby), is just reaching that stage now; so far, when she touches something forbidden and we say "No!" she stops and looks at us in wide-eyed wonder. The possibility of defying us hasn't yet occurred to her, but any day now it will.

But by the time that happens you don't have a baby; you have a toddler. And if babies are naturally pure and innocent, toddlers are something else altogether.

If you're not a parent, you probably have heard of the "terrible twos" and are wondering if it's even worthwhile having children. If you are a parent of a child over 2, you probably don't need to read the next few paragraphs—you could have written them.

As Christopher grew through his terrible twos, he changed in many ways. He still loved to laugh and play. He grew even more fascinated with music and began playing his toy guitar, his toy violin, and his toy saxophone. And he learned to talk, which greatly increased his ability to interact with people. Now he could actually say, "Look at me! I'm cute!"

But along with all these positive developments, his stubbornness and strong will increased too. He developed the classic toddler love affair with "No!" And he developed the ability to complain, to argue, even to be rude if he chose to.

My aunt has a dog who, like Christopher, has a naturally lively, outgoing personality. Some days, when the dog (who is now getting old) is tired or lazy or bored, my aunt will say, "Poor Mindy; she's not herself." This has become a catchphrase with the rest of the family—most of us not being as closely attuned to the dog's moods as my aunt is. We'll ask teasingly, "How's Mindy? Is she herself?"

More Like Myself

That's kind of how I feel about Christopher when he's having a stubborn, negative, toddler kind of day. He's not "himself." Now, a casual observer might conclude that he's stubborn and negative so much of the time that this actually is himself—this is what he's normally like. But I know better. I've known him since he was born, since he was (for all intents and purposes) perfect and sinless, so I know what his real warm sunny personality is like.

So as Christopher moves through that fierce struggle for independence that is toddlerhood, I focus on and enjoy those moments when he is happy, sunny, and loving. I cherish the times when he says, "I love you, Mommy!" and the delight he takes in trying out primitive jokes to make us laugh. I love to watch as he entertains his baby sister or dances around the room with his guitar, music playing full blast, lost in the joy of movement. At those moments I can see that he is truly himself—the self he started out to be, the self he will grow into once we help him steer through the treacherous rapids of 2 and 3 and whatever lies beyond.

We can debate till our mouths are dry about whether human beings are inherently good or inherently evil, and find plenty of evidence to support either claim. We cannot deny the reality of sin, nor of the sinfulness of human nature, yet neither can we deny the glorious reality that we were created in the image of God.

Some people see religion, Christianity, as a process of shaping and molding us into something we were never meant to be, some creature quite different from ourselves. I have never been able to see it that way. Grasping the truth that we were created in God's image, I have always felt intuitively what I now see acted out in my child's life—that sin robs us of ourselves, makes us less than what we truly are, less than what God intended us to be. When we put ourselves in the hands of the One who made us in the first place, He chips away the stubbornness and the negativity and the disobedience to reveal the shining, smiling, lovely creature He created in the first place.

It's easy to mix this up with the New Age idea that we are all divine, all gods within. In fact, I think that's why this idea is so popular and has such appeal—because, despite all the sin and depravity around us, we still recognize so much beauty, creativity, and joy in human nature, in ourselves, that we want to believe we are really like that on the inside, really perfect.

Unfortunately for the New Age, it's hard to explain how someone who is divine within can commit serial murder or rape or even the thousand casual injuries we all inflict on others every day. But if we recognize that the beauty within does not come from ourselves, but from the divine Maker who left His mark on us, we can accept that only through His power will we ever again recapture that original perfect image.

As Christopher grows past the terrible twos (as I write this, he's one month into what I've been told should be called the trying threes), I can see more and more moments when his true sunny nature emerges from underneath the facade of "No! I don't wanna!" I cherish the moments when I see him becoming more and more like himself. And I pray too that in the hands of my God, I also am becoming daily more like myself.

God created man in his own image, in the image of God he created him; male and female he created them. Genesis 1:27, NIV.

THINK IT THROUGH

1. How do you balance the question of good and evil in human nature? Do you think of yourself as essentially a sinful being or essentially a perfect creation of God?

2. If we are created in God's image, why do we so strongly resist becoming more like Him?

3. In what moments of your life are you most truly "yourself"? Have you sensed God's presence in those moments?

28.

"WE DON'T NEED JESUS, MOMMY"

Four-year-old Scott had been sick for days. He was running a high fever and had a bad cough. His mom, Joanne, had tried all the usual home remedies, but nothing seemed to work, and this was dragging on longer than she liked. She wanted a doctor to see Scott.

This wasn't as easy for her as it was for many mothers of small children. She and her husband were serving in the mission field. There was a good doctor in the community who was also a good friend of theirs, but he was often traveling to other villages, holding clinics in remote areas where medical care was hard to come by. Joanne would have called Dr. Jim days ago, but he had been away.

That morning at breakfast, when she said, "I'm still worried about Scott's fever," her husband said, "Well, at least you can call Jim now. He got back late last night."

What a relief! Joanne immediately called Jim, and he agreed to come have a look at Scott right after breakfast. Then she went up to the room where her feverish little boy was still sleeping. She sat beside him, a hand on his small hot forehead, till he stirred and awoke.

"How are you feeling, sweetheart?"

Scott smiled that cute smile that always melted her heart. Even when he was sick and cranky he was such a sweet kid. "I'm OK,

Mommy." He coughed. "But my throat still hurts."

"Well, I just talked to Dr. Jim, and he's going to come visit you. He'll probably want to look in your throat and your ears, and listen to your chest, and he might give you some medicine."

"Oh, good!" Scott liked Dr. Jim, even though Dr. Jim had given him shots.

"Do you want anything to eat?"

"No," said Scott in a tired voice. "I want some juice."

"OK, I'll go get some juice. But first, why don't we pray to Jesus?" Joanne tried to start each morning by having a little prayer with Scott; lately she'd been praying each morning that Jesus would make Scott feel better.

Scott frowned. "But Mommy, we don't need Jesus to make me better. Dr. Jim's coming!"

Joanne thought a lot about that comment as she went down to get juice. Of course she'd explained that they still needed Jesus and had gone ahead with prayer. But it bothered her how easily her son assumed that God was dispensable as soon as human help was available. She was still thinking about it after Dr. Jim left, leaving behind a prescription for the antibiotics Scott needed. And a few days later, when Scott was again up and lively and bouncing off the walls, Joanne hadn't forgotten the comment.

We automatically assume that whatever comes out of a small child's mouth is a reflection of what he or she has seen and heard—usually at home, if that's where the child spends most of his or her time. Children really are sponges. They do soak up our attitudes and our opinions. So Joanne wondered if Scott's comment was a childish mistake, or a reflection of her own attitude. Yes, she'd prayed to Jesus every day, but she hadn't really felt at peace about Scott's illness until she knew the doctor was available. Had she somehow failed to make it clear to Scott—or to herself—that Dr. Jim was just an instrument in God's hand to help them? Did she really believe that if Dr. Jim had stayed out of town, God would still have been in control of what happened to Scott?

In *Mere Christianity* C. S. Lewis writes: "You may say 'I've never had the sense of being helped by an invisible Christ, but I often have been helped by other human beings.' That is rather like the woman in the first [world] war who said that if there were a bread shortage it would not bother her house because they always ate toast. If there is no bread there will be no toast. If there were no help from Christ, there would be no help from other human beings. He works on us in all sorts of ways. But above all, He works on us through each other."

Her son's innocent comment made Joanne wonder if she'd been eating toast without recognizing the Loaf from which it was cut. I wondered the same thing when she told me the story. I can pray to God endlessly for help with a particular situation, yet when human help arrives, I somehow don't connect it with my prayers. It's harder than I'd like to admit, not only to recognize God as the source of all human help, but also as the One who will be there when no human help comes, when every other hope has vanished, when He's all we have left to cling to.

> **God is our refuge and strength, an ever-present help in trouble. Therefore we will not fear, though the earth give way and the mountains fall into the heart of the sea, though its waters roar and foam and the mountains quake with their surging. Psalm 46:1-3, NIV.**

THINK IT THROUGH

1. Can you think of a time in your life God has helped you through another human being? Can you think of a time He has helped you when no human help was available?

2. How confident do you feel when you know you have only God to rely on?

29.

LOST SHEEP

Terry was a handful. For Leslie, a 22-year-old first-year teacher in a small multigrade church school, Terry was the kind of third grader she had nightmares about.

Terry didn't listen. Terry didn't like to sit still. Terry didn't do his work. Terry yelled and talked back and hit other kids. Terry seemed to spend his entire educational career either sitting in time-out or staying after class.

Terry's father was the pastor. His mother had already given Leslie a few lectures about things she didn't think the new teacher was doing properly, and that made it even harder to deal with Terry.

Leslie had a lot of tension headaches.

None of the strategies Leslie had learned in her education classes the previous year seemed to apply to Terry. The chapters on discipline, motivation, and handling problem students had seemed so easy when she was the one sitting in the classroom, reading her textbook and writing papers. She had gotten straight A's in her project on motivating the troublesome child. But now, on the other side of the desk, she felt she was failing miserably with Terry.

She tried. She planned. She even prayed. But mostly she just wished Terry's father would get a call in the middle of the year to pastor some other church. She liked him as a pastor. But if he left, Terry would go. And that was what Leslie wanted most of all—no Terry.

Then one day, quite unexpectedly, her wish came true.

Lost Sheep

The schoolroom was in the basement of the church building, on the outskirts of town. Outside were fields, woods, a stream. It was a beautiful spring day, and Leslie and all her students were outside playing during recess. When recess time ended, Leslie blew her whistle, and the children trooped back into the classroom.

Class had been in session for about 15 minutes when Leslie noticed that Terry wasn't in his seat. She glanced around the room, but he wasn't there. "Has anyone seen Terry?" she asked. "Did he come back in after recess?"

The children shook their heads. "No, I don't think he came in," several little voices chorused.

Leslie stormed outside, muttering under her breath. This was just the last straw—that little troublemaker staying outside to play, disrupting class, disobeying her again. *This time I really will call his parents,* she thought. *I don't care what they say.*

Terry was not in the field behind the church. He was nowhere near the building. Leslie strode across the meadow to the trees beyond. "Terry!" she called sharply. There was no reply. She went deeper into the woods, calling his name again and again.

Leslie stood under the trees, looking around. Terry had been missing—she checked her watch—nearly a half hour. This child could be anywhere. She tried not to picture him facedown in the stream. Her heart tightened.

"Terry! Terry!" There was a note of panic in her voice now.

Leslie was running by this time, through the woods, back toward the church. Some of the children were standing outside now. "Miss Evans! Did you find Terry? Where is he? We'll help you look!" The children joined Leslie, calling Terry's name over and over. Leslie tried to hide her fear. She couldn't let them know how serious this was.

But she would have to let another adult know, and quickly. It was time to tell the principal—if he hadn't already noticed the children running around behind the building yelling Terry's name. Leslie went back into the church basement. Some of the children followed her. They were quiet by now, sensing that this was more than just a joke on Terry's part.

Lord, please let him be all right. Dear Lord, please don't let Terry be dead or hurt. Leslie didn't even know how long she had been praying this prayer—it was just part of her thoughts.

On her way back to the classroom she passed the furnace room. A slight rustling sound from inside caught her attention. She pulled open the door and switched on the light in the hot, pitch-black room.

Terry was behind the furnace. Hiding. Doubled over with laughter. His trick had worked better than he could have hoped.

It might have been the moment to give Terry the punishment of his life. Some of the other children certainly thought that. "Oooohh, Terry, you're in trouble now," they breathed excitedly.

Years later Leslie, a lifelong veteran of the teaching profession, doesn't even remember whether she punished Terry for his prank. What she does remember, she says, is "the relief that flooded through my body upon finding him. I was angry and delighted at the same time. How important he had become to me in the 45 or so minutes he had been missing."

Leslie prayed a new prayer that night—simply that she would love Terry as much as she loved the other 20 children in her class. That she would always see Terry's value as clearly as she did when he was missing.

Terry didn't become a better child during those 45 minutes. In fact, he was as bad as he'd ever been, or worse, while he was hiding out in the furnace room. What changed during those 45 minutes was Leslie's perspective. She saw Terry as a valuable human being. As his parents saw him. As God saw him. As God, perhaps, sees us all.

Maybe the lost sheep, sheep number 100, was the problem sheep in the flock. Maybe the other 99 were cute and cuddly and easy to love. Maybe number 100 had a goatlike temperament instead of being properly sheepish. It certainly makes sense that way if we understand the parable of the lost sheep to be not only about every lost sinner, but about our lost world, the one unlovable rebel among all the well-behaved planets in God's universe.

The shepherd Jesus talked about didn't go searching for his best sheep, or his prize sheep, or his smartest sheep. He just searched for the missing one. Because it mattered. Because it had value.

Leslie's prayer about Terry was answered—as was the same

prayer when she prayed it dozens of times in the years to come, over dozens of students who were unlovable, unfriendly, unpromising, sometimes even unclean. Leslie found she could love Terry. And Terry's behavior really did change as a result of that love. Leslie found she could love any child, no matter how badly behaved, when she saw them through God's eyes—the Shepherd's eyes.

Suppose one of you has a hundred sheep and loses one of them. Does he not leave the ninety-nine in the open country and go after the lost sheep until he finds it? And when he finds it, he joyfully puts it on his shoulders and goes home. Then he calls his friends and neighbors together and says, "Rejoice with me; I have found my lost sheep." I tell you that in the same way there will be more rejoicing in heaven over one sinner who repents than over ninety-nine righteous persons who do not need to repent. Luke 15:4-7, NIV.

THINK IT THROUGH

1. What would it take for you to be able to see an unlovely, unattractive person through God's eyes?

2. Do you ever see yourself in the role of the lost sheep? Is it difficult for you to appreciate the value God has placed on you? How can you begin seeing yourself through God's eyes?

30.

THIS IS YOUR LIFE

In Thornton Wilder's play *Our Town* Emily Webb, a young woman who dies in childbirth, is given the chance to come back to earth and relive one day of her life in the small town of Grover's Corners, New Hampshire.

Of course, as an Adventist reader, you'll recognize immediately that this is an inaccurate portrayal of the state of the dead, but like Jesus' parable of the rich man and Lazarus, *Our Town* is not really about death at all. It's about life and how we live it.

Emily chooses to relive the day of her twelfth birthday. Standing in her own kitchen as an invisible spectator, she mourns as she sees how she and her loved ones took for granted the ordinary, everyday moments of a life that now seems unspeakably precious to her.

"I didn't realize," Emily says. "So all that was going on and we never noticed. . . . Goodbye, world. Goodbye, Grover's Corners . . . Mama and Papa. Goodbye to clocks ticking . . . and Mama's sunflowers. And food and coffee. And new-ironed dresses and hot baths . . . and sleeping and waking up. Oh, earth, you're too wonderful for anybody to realize you."

As she turns away from her one day back on earth, unable to bear it, Emily asks the Stage Manager, "Do any human beings ever realize life while they live it—every, every minute?"

And the Stage Manager answers, "No. The saints and poets, maybe—they do some."

This Is Your Life

Once you have children, the most unbearable thought on earth is that death may snatch one of them from you. I would hate to be Emily Webb's mother. And I would hate to think that if one of my children was taken from me, and could somehow come back and watch a day from his or her own life, I would be seen ignoring the joy of the present moment, failing to appreciate the wonderful living child I have in front of me.

Wilder's play suggests that only the most deeply spiritual and creative human beings have the ability to actually appreciate life as it passes by. The rest of us are doomed to look back and sigh, "Where did the time go? I was happy back then . . . why didn't I realize it?"

I first read *Our Town* in my late teens, and this scene hit me with shattering force and forever rearranged the way I view the world. The poignancy of Emily's too-late realization of life's beauty made me determine that I was not going to be one of the ordinary folks who let life slip past. I would recognize and appreciate life when I had it—I would be either a saint or a poet.

A decade and a half later I'm making my living as a professional writer, but definitely not a poet. And as for sainthood—well, I'm far from achieving it if you accept the popular definition of a saint as someone who is holier than everyone else around. But according to the New Testament definition, every believer is a saint, and I firmly believe that every Christian can overcome the human tendency to take life for granted. Every one of us can do what Wilder said only saints and poets could do—we can all stop, take a deep breath, and really notice our lives while we are living them. It's the best thing we can do for ourselves.

Like so many other life truths, this one comes home with additional force now that I have children. Lately the lyrics of a song by contemporary Christian artist David Kauffman have been making me cry every time I turn on the radio. It's called "Turn Around Slowly."

> *I met a grandfather and all of his children*
> *And as we were talking a tear filled his eye*
> *He smiled at my child, I handed her to him*
> *And just for a moment, he went back in time*

He remembered the dreams of having a family
Of holding the ones that God sent his way
The joy they would bring him to make his heart larger
Then he looked in my eyes and said

Turn around slowly, time is a racer
The wink of an eye takes you from here to there
Turn around slowly and treasure your days here
These precious moments may come to an end

In a flash he discovered my foolish wishes
I wish she was walking and talking and more
But why hurry what will pass me so quickly
I should be longing to linger

And held in his arms my child turned back to me
As if to say listen well
She said look at me Daddy and love me this moment
This moment is all that we have . . . she said

Turn around slowly, time is a racer
The wink of an eye takes you from here to there
Turn around slowly and treasure your days here
These precious moments may come to an end★

It's the ultimate truth in child raising—you have so little time; cherish every moment. But it's not only true of children. It's true of marriage, of friendships, of your parents, of every important relationship and, indeed, every daily moment in life. This moment is all that we have.

Most people live their lives in a blur, harried by deadlines, focused on some imaginary future. Some may look toward that future with hope and ambition, others with fear or dread, but both are missing the point. They are ignoring the present reality and investing everything in the future. Planning ahead is useful to a point, but the Bible reminds us that we can't count on the future. Like the rich fool, who died in his sleep after planning to expand his warehouses, we may hear the ringing words, "You fool! This very night your life will be demanded from you. Then who will get what you have prepared for yourself?" (Luke 12:20, NIV).

The problem is that most of us live our lives as if they are a dress rehearsal for the "real" life we're going to live later on. Students think, *I can't wait till I graduate and get a job!* Young adults think, *Once I find the right person and get married, then I'll be happy,* or, *When I can get out of this job and find a better one, I'll be content.* Parents struggling to raise their families think, *When the kids are a little older . . . when they're in school . . . when they leave home, then I'll have time to enjoy myself."* And too many elderly people find themselves in the middle of those retirement years, looking back and wondering, *How did life slip by so quickly?*

One realization can transform your outlook: this is your life. This is your real life, and it's the only one you're going to get on this earth. The job you do, the place you live, the family you have—or don't have—this is your reality, right now. Accept it, and live it.

This doesn't mean that you don't strive for something better, if the life you have now is unsatisfactory. In fact, it means just the opposite. If there are things about your life right now that are genuinely bad for you, don't waste time daydreaming about a "someday" when they'll be better. This is your life, right now—so do what you have to do to make it work for you. If things aren't going well in your marriage, maybe it's time to sit down and talk to your spouse or make an appointment to see a counselor. If the relationship is abusive, it's time to get out and start respecting this one life that you have been given.

If your job is frustrating, don't while away your hours fantasizing about retirement. Do what you need to do to make that job better for you—or haul out your résumé and start seriously looking for another one.

Don't wait for the perfect life you're going to get someday, down the road. This is your life. Do what you need to do to make it a good one for you, right now.

And while you're taking care of those big things, stop and notice the little things. Sometimes the life we're living is pretty much the one we've always dreamed of, but we don't appreciate it because we're too busy, too focused on our long-term goals, to really live it.

While I worked on this article, 2½-year-old Christopher sat on my bed, wrapped up in blankets, with his teddy bear. "I got to go on my boat!" he said. "Do you want to come on my boat?"

It would have been easy to ignore him, to say, "No, I'm working on the computer—you and Teddy Bear enjoy the boat ride." Instead, I saved my file and went from the computer to the bed, sat down, and got on the boat ride. We sang "Row, row, row your boat," and "Rock, rock, rock, little boat on the sparkling sea." For 10 minutes I shared an imaginary boat ride with the most creative, interesting person I know, and I immersed myself fully in that moment, that experience. I didn't do it so that Christopher would someday remember and care that his mother took time to play with him instead of working—though I hope he will remember that. I did it mostly for myself. Because this is the life I chose to live, being at home with my children, and if I'm not experiencing it fully, if I don't "turn around slowly," then I'm cheating myself.

I make a habit of stopping often in the middle of family activities to say "I'm so happy right now!" My husband always finds this a little surprising, but I've explained to him that when I feel happy, when I notice that I'm enjoying myself, I want to announce it, to celebrate it. I don't want that moment to slip past and be forgotten.

Emily Webb had her list of precious things she didn't notice till it was too late: clocks and sunflowers, new-ironed dresses, and hot baths. What's on your list? Look around at your home, your life, your world. What are the sights, the sounds, the smells that you would miss if they were gone? Who are the people who make your life worth celebrating? Take note of those people, those things. And then give yourself a few minutes each day just to enjoy them.

Wear the dress that makes you feel beautiful. Cook the meal you love to taste (or go out to a restaurant for it!). Play the music you love at top volume on your stereo. Rock your baby even after she falls asleep. Spend a half hour just talking with a loved family member or friend—no agenda, just conversation. Take that walk. Work in the garden. Read that book. And while you're enjoying these things, pay attention. Tell yourself, "I love this, and I'm taking time for it because I love it."

Most of all, take time for God. Time just to be with Him—not to serve on a church committee or prepare for teaching a Sabbath school class, but to open your heart in prayer. God is not one more component of a happy life; He's the center, the person around whom it all revolves. Remember Jesus' advice not to worry about tomorrow? We don't worry, we don't focus all our hopes and energies on the future, because we're seeking God *today*. Putting Him first. Living and appreciating the wonderful life He's given us.

This is your life. Live it.

> **Seek first [God's] kingdom and his righteousness, and all these things will be given to you as well. Therefore do not worry about tomorrow, for tomorrow will worry about itself. Each day has enough trouble of its own. Matthew 6:33, 34, NIV.**

THINK IT THROUGH

1. Are you mostly focused on the life you're living right now, or on some future goal? Does this need to change?

2. How do we balance the need to plan and prepare for the future with the need to appreciate the present moment?

---

*Words and music by David Kauffman. Copyright 1999 David Kauffman Songs. To purchase SIMPLE TRUTH, on which is found the song, "Turn Around Slowly," go to davidkauffman.com. To contact David, call 1-800-759-5805, or write david@davidkauffman.com.

MENTORS

When I was planning this book, I thought it might be nice to include a section about mentors—the people who have influenced you, who have helped you grow into the person you are today. I had this neat story about my old Pathfinder counselor ("Kari's Gift"—you'll get to it in just a few minutes), and I thought, *There's got to be tons more stories like that out there. Surely everyone has a mentor they have fond memories of.*

Well, maybe they do, but they sure weren't sharing them with me. From my entire circle of friends and acquaintances whom I tackled for this book I received not one story about a mentor. Finally I started asking specifically for such stories, and got my dad's story about his guitar teacher, and my friend's story about a piece of advice his high school principal gave him. Apart from that, nothing.

Now I've probably done it—I'll be flooded with calls and e-mail from people saying, "Why, my tenth-grade biology teacher was such an influence in my life . . ." Sorry, folks; the book is written. I'll admit I didn't do any kind of scientific survey, and my sample was pretty small. But I wonder whether maybe there isn't enough mentoring going on out there—or whether people aren't taking the time to reflect on and appreciate those who helped them along the way.

Whatever the cause, I still liked the concept, because I think God works through these people in our lives—those who aren't

147

blood relatives but who are in our lives just because they care about us, people who are a little older and wiser and a little further along the way than we are. So I've shared a couple stories about my own mentors and the few stories I did pick up from others, and one about my own unplanned attempt to be a mentor to one of my students. If any of this jogs your memory and makes you want to write a thank-you note to someone who mentored you, that's great. And if it jogs your conscience and makes you say, "Hey, I really should accept that offer to teach earliteen Sabbath School—maybe I could be someone's mentor!" well, that's great too. Praise the Lord.

31.

KARI'S GIFT

L ike many small churches, my childhood church had an on-again, off-again Pathfinder Club. I dimly recall some Pathfinder activities when I was 8 or 9, but then the club lay dormant for lack of leadership for several years. The year I was 14 and in grade 9 some brave adults decided to revive the club, and every kid in church joined.

I was in the Explorer unit with my two classmates, Suzanne and Deena, and Suzanne's sister Barbara, who was a year older than we were. We were the oldest girls in the club, and our counselor was Kari, who seemed very mature to me at the time but who was probably in her early 20s.

Kari was a newcomer to our area. She and her husband had moved there when he became manager of our Adventist radio station. We didn't know Kari very well when the Pathfinder year began, and we were a little shy of her.

That didn't last long. Kari was the kind of young woman that teenage girls love to idolize—she was pretty and soft-spoken but funny, she could sing, she invited us to her house, and she treated us like real human beings.

I didn't realize at the time how much of a challenge that last part was. Suzanne, Deena, and I were friends not only because we were the only three Adventist girls in our class at school, but also because we had a lot in common: we were all smart in school, extremely talkative, quite energetic, and moderately rebellious.

Only moderately. We laughed at Pathfinder Investiture when they gave out good conduct ribbons. All three of us knew we were not going to be in the running for good conduct ribbons; we would have been faintly ashamed if we had gotten them. But we weren't serious candidates for bad conduct ribbons, either. We didn't smoke or swear or cheat on tests. We were the kind of rebels who wouldn't shut up in class and talked back to the teachers and giggled helplessly during Pathfinder drill exercises because we got our left and right mixed up—sometimes on purpose.

Suzanne's sister Barbara was another story. She was quiet and gentle, barely spoke above a whisper, and seemed to always do exactly what adults expected of her. I didn't dislike her at all; it just seemed as if she were an entirely different sort of creature from me.

Kari and her husband were newlyweds and, so far, didn't have any kids of their own. We teased her endlessly about having children and suggested she ought to have 12. "And name some of them after us," we'd say.

"OK," she told us repeatedly, "I'll have 12 girls. I'll have a Suzanne, a Deena, a Trudy, and nine Barbaras!"

We knew we drove her crazy, but we also knew she liked us. She put a lot of time and effort into our Pathfinder program—she even helped sew our uniform skirts. She taught us all the words to a song she sang for special music, which we absolutely loved ("Requiem for a Little Boy"—I've listened to it on a scratchy old 33 record since then, trying to recapture the magic it held when Kari's voice sang the words and Kari's fingers picked out the accompaniment on her guitar). And she survived a weekend camporee in which we tried with enthusiastic though doomed determination to win the award for best all-around unit.

At the end of that year Kari and her husband moved away. Suzanne, Deena, Barbara, and I were all crushed. We wanted to continue in Pathfinders for another year, but we couldn't imagine how we would go on without Kari as our counselor. We pleaded with her not to leave, not quite comprehending how her own life could be so important to her when we needed her right there in the Pathfinder Club.

Kari's Gift

At our last unit meeting of the year Kari gave each of us gifts she had bought. Three of them were fair-sized wrapped packages: those were for Suzanne, Deena, and Barbara, though I don't recall what they got. I know she had chosen a different gift for each person, one that seemed perfectly suited to the individual.

My gift was only an envelope. Inside a card was a homemade crossword puzzle. "Do the puzzle," Kari said, "and it'll tell you what your gift is."

Quickly I worked the puzzle, with lots of help and advice from the other girls. Only one clue was difficult: "A deep-sea prescription," 12 letters.

"Sorry; that's not a very good clue, but it was a really hard word to think of a clue for," Kari said. She gave me a few hints. Finally I filled it in: *subscription*. I sorted out the words in their correct order: *A year's subscription to* Writer's Digest.

Kari knew that my dream was to be a writer. Well, actually everyone knew it—it wasn't something I was shy or secretive about. But not everyone took it seriously—being a writer, after all, isn't considered a realistic career choice for most people. I hadn't realized until I opened Kari's gift how much she believed in me, in my potential to fulfill that dream.

Kari's gift didn't actually begin arriving until she had gone. When the monthly issues of *Writer's Digest* starting arriving in my mailbox, I devoured every one. This was a real magazine, a magazine for grown-up professional writers. About 80 percent of it was way over my head at the time, but that made me enjoy it all the more. It gave me a sense that there was a real and serious world out there of writing and being published that I would someday enter. And here I am.

Only now, as an adult, does the generosity of Kari's gift really take my breath away. Not that a year's subscription to *Writer's Digest* is so very expensive—though it probably cost more than I've ever spent on a year-end gift for anyone in my Pathfinder unit. Rather, it was her generosity of spirit that amazes me—her thoughtfulness in choosing gifts that suited each one of her four temperamental Pathfinders, her love for me despite the fact that I never qualified for a good conduct ribbon, her willingness to see and affirm my dreams with a gift that invited me into the adult world.

We need so much more of that generosity of spirit—I've needed it often in my life as a teacher, a youth leader, a Pathfinder counselor, an adult. To tell a younger person, "I believe in you. Your dreams matter, and I think you'll achieve them"—that's an incredible gift. Help me, Lord, to give someone that kind of a gift.

**Where there is no vision, the people perish.
Proverbs 29:18, KJV.**

THINK IT THROUGH

1. What were your childhood dreams? Did the adults in your life affirm them or belittle them?

2. Has anyone ever given you a gift like Kari's?

3. Is there a younger person in your life to whom you can give that kind of gift?

32.

SUNDAY AFTERNOONS

When Allan Martin was a student at a boarding academy Sunday afternoons were among his favorite times of the week. His work supervisor, Mr. K, made a hobby of visiting flea markets and yard sales, searching for secondhand treasures. A couple times he invited Allan to join him at the flea markets on Sunday, and soon it became a tradition.

Allan didn't become a bona fide flea market maniac like Mr. K. He didn't unearth a valuable antique for only $5 and later sell it on the *Antiques Roadshow* for $250,000. But he did gain something priceless from that weekly appointment—something many teenagers never get. He got the undivided attention of a caring adult on a regular basis. Even one hour a week of that kind of attention can make a huge difference.

Now an adult specializing in youth and young adult ministry, Allan Martin says, "Beyond being my work supervisor, Mr. K was my friend and a wonderful support during the turbulent years of adolescence. His simple gift hour to me was a vivid reminder that I was not alone." [1]

In his essay, Allan Martin challenges adults to "give at least an hour of your time each week to relationship with a Generation X young person. Niche out an intentional, uninterrupted segment of quality time to be spent relationally with an Xer or with a baby buster family." [2]

CONNECTING

You may see yourself on either side of this equation. Perhaps you've had older adults who took the time to spend an hour a week—or more—with you during a critical time of your life. Maybe you're grateful to someone who mentored you when you needed them. Or perhaps you've never experienced that and wish you had. Maybe there's an older, more experienced teacher, coworker, family member, or church friend that you can cultivate that kind of relationship with. Lots of people are afraid to reach out to a younger person for fear they'll be rejected. Let them know you need them.

Look in the other direction, too—at those younger than you, those post-Gen Xers that nobody's even found a good generational name for yet. The teenagers. The Pathfinders. The high school students. The younger siblings. Is there someone there you can spare a gift hour for?

What I like about Allan's story of Mr. K and the flea markets is that Mr. K didn't pull up a chair and say, "Allan, tell me what's going on in your life." That approach would probably freeze any teenager into an instant ice sculpture. Most of us don't like to be confronted head-on with relationship. We like relationship to ease its way in around the edges of daily activities.

I've spent most of my adult life—almost from the moment I left my teens—working with teenagers. In those years I've had some fantastically meaningful, eye-opening conversations and "teachable moments" with my students and youth group members. Very few of them, however, have come about as the result of a deliberate attempt to sit down and "relate." There's an essay elsewhere in this book called "I Don't Know What to Say," in which you'll find that one of the most meaningful conversations I've had recently with anyone in my church youth group occurred while sweeping the floor and yelling at the top of our lungs to be heard above the background music.

Sweeping floors, trolling flea markets for unexpected treasure, building model rockets, playing soccer—these are the activities, the moments, when connection occurs. When we touch someone else's life and allow someone to touch ours. Sometimes we're not even aware it's happening, until we look back and see how the shape of a life has been changed by an impression we made.

> **Teach the older men to be temperate, worthy of respect, self-controlled, and sound in faith, in love and in endurance. Likewise, teach the older women to be reverent in the way they live . . . to teach what is good. Then they can train the younger women. . . . Similarly, encourage the young men to be self-controlled. In everything set them an example by doing what is good. Titus 2:2-7, NIV.**

THINK IT THROUGH

1. The verse above from Paul's letter to Titus pictures a community of faith in which older and younger members work together in mutual respect, with the youth learning from older mentors. Was this kind of community a reality in the church in which you grew up, or in the church you now attend? Do you know of any nonchurch groups or communities in which this kind of mentoring goes on?

2. Did anyone in your youth take time for you as Mr. K did for Allan? Is there a tangible way in which you can thank that person now, if you haven't done so already?

3. How can you accept the challenge to mentor someone younger?

---

[1] A. Allan Martin, "The Gift Hour." I originally found this essay online at http://www.tagnet.org/dvm/gifthour/html; it has since been adapted for the book *Unleash the Dream*, compiled by Andy Nash and published by the Review and Herald.
[2] *Ibid.*

33.

"DON'T WORRY ABOUT THE MONEY"

In his last year of high school Mike had the chance to go on a mission trip to the Dominican Republic. He was excited about the trip, and after talking it over with his parents, teachers, and friends, he decided to go for it. The $1,300 he would have to raise for the trip seemed like a huge barrier, but several people assured him he would probably get some significant sponsorship from his home church, so that would make it a little easier.

Mike began fund-raising, planning, and preparing for the trip. He also put in a request to his church board asking for support. But for some reason, his request was denied. As is so often the case, there was a lot of politics involved that Mike, as a young person, didn't fully understand. Three youth from that church were joining the trip, and the church board couldn't seem to agree about which, if any, of them were going to get sponsored.

For Mike, the bottom line was clear: he wasn't getting any money. He had counted on a few hundred dollars from the church. Now his goal seemed so distant as to be impossible. Over the next few days and weeks he thought it over and even prayed about it, but he had to admit he didn't see where he could raise that kind of money. Certainly his parents didn't have that kind of cash to hand over.

"Don't Worry About the Money"

One day the academy principal stopped Mike in the hall between classes. "How's it going, Mike?" Mr. Sellars asked.

"OK, I guess," Mike said.

"How's the fund-raising for your trip coming?"

"Oh, uh, I've decided not to go on the trip," Mike said.

"Really?" Of course the academy principal had a pretty good idea of what went on behind closed doors in church board meetings, and he'd heard that Mike hadn't gotten the funding he'd hoped for. Still, Mr. Sellars asked, "Why is that?"

"Well, I just don't see where I can get the money from. It's way too much, and my folks can't afford it."

Mr. Sellars nodded. "I can see where that would worry you, Mike. But you know what I think?"

"What's that, sir?"

"I think you shouldn't worry about the money. If it's a good cause, if this is something the Lord wants you to do, the money will come from somewhere. I've seen people set out on projects like this again and again, and I assure you, the money always comes from somewhere. God will provide it."

Mike looked—and felt—a little skeptical. But the principal seemed so sure. "Go ahead and make your plans, Mike, as if you were going on the trip. I believe God will make it happen. Don't worry about the money."

Mike took Mr. Sellars' advice. He went home and told his parents he was still planning to go on the trip, he was still going to keep fund-raising, and he was going to trust God to provide the money.

God came through—in the form of several generous gifts from friends, family, and church members who believed Mike deserved the chance to go on the mission trip. Mike went and had a wonderful two weeks, which even today he still remembers as a highlight of his teenage years.

He still remembers Mr. Sellars' advice, too. Don't worry about the money—go ahead and plan. If God wants it to happen, He'll send the money.

I knew both Mike and Mr. Sellars at the time this happened, and I'm pretty sure Mr. Sellars didn't have $1,300 in his back pocket to pull out and give to Mike. I don't even know if Mr. Sellars himself was able to make any financial contribution to Mike's mission trip fund, though he probably did. If he had been rich enough to pay Mike's whole way, this would have been a wonderful story about generosity, but as it stands, it's a wonderful story about faith. What Mr. Sellars had to give Mike was not $1,300, but the faith that God could provide $1,300—or any other amount Mike might need.

"Don't worry about the money"—or about any of those other annoying details that trip us up and bog us down—is difficult advice to follow, but it's advice God has been giving His people ever since Jesus said, "Seek first the kingdom of God, and all these things will be added to you." He delivers that message to us over and over in many different ways; to Mike, He delivered it through a teacher who had had occasion to learn a little about faith, trust, and the God of the impossible.

Do not worry about your life, what you will eat or drink; or about your body, what you will wear. Is not life more important than food, and the body more important than clothes? Look at the birds of the air; they do not sow or reap or store away in barns, and yet your heavenly Father feeds them. Are you not much more valuable than they? Who of you by worrying can add a single hour to his life? And why do you worry about clothes? See how the lilies of the field grow. They do not labor or spin. Yet I tell you that not even Solomon in all his splendor was dressed like one of these. If that is how God clothes the grass of the field, which is here today and tomorrow is thrown into the fire, will he not much more clothe you, O you of little faith? So do not worry, saying, "What shall we eat?" or "What shall we drink?" or "What shall we wear?" For the pagans run after all these things, and your

**heavenly Father knows that you need them. But
seek first his kingdom and his righteousness, and
all these things will be given to you as well.
Therefore do not worry about tomorrow, for
tomorrow will worry about itself. Each day has
enough trouble of its own. Matthew 6:25-34, NIV.**

THINK IT THROUGH

1. What do you worry about? What worries do you find it hardest to let go of?

2. Has God ever proved His ability to do the impossible in your life? When and how?

3. Do you have enough faith in God's ability to provide that you, like Mr. Sellars, could tell someone else not to worry about money? Does it take more faith to apply God's promises to yourself or to someone else? Why?

34.

SPRING AND FALL

When I was in university, one of my heros was the assistant girls' dean. Vicky was a single woman who turned 30 while I lived in the dorm—I know this because she sent me and several friends an invitation to her thirtieth birthday party, with the explanation that "turning 30 gets a lot of bad press—but when you consider the alternatives, i.e., never reaching 30 or skipping directly to 31, I consider it something to celebrate." Of course she seemed quite old to me at the time, but she was quick, witty, a good listener, and good company.

My friends and I spent a lot of her on-duty evenings hanging around her office, talking and laughing. Though she didn't quite treat us as equals—because we were always aware that she was older than we were and in authority over us—we always respected her. I suppose she just treated us as people. As though she actually enjoyed being around us.

We certainly enjoyed being around her. One of my favorite memories is of an evening when three friends and I stayed up late in Vicky's office, talking with her till finally all of us, Vicky included, got very hyper and giggly and loud. The resident assistant from the floor above us had to come down and ask us to be quiet—probably one of the few times in dorm history an RA had to ask the dean to keep her office quiet!

Vicky was also an excellent role model as a well-adjusted, happy

Spring and Fall

single woman at a time in our lives when most of us girls were quite focused on finding Mr. Right. Once, giving a dorm worship talk, she told the story of a man she knew who was advised to put an avocado pit in a glass of water so he could watch it sprout. Having done so, he pulled up a chair in front of the glass and started watching, apparently assuming it was an instantaneous phenomenon. A friend patted him on the shoulder and said, "One word of advice— do something while you wait." That, she said, was her advice to us—do something while you wait for marriage, something like living your life, rather than sitting around watching for the knight on the white horse.

One evening during my senior year my current knight had ridden away on his white horse with the infamous parting words "I think we should see other people." I went to my best friend's room to weep and wail and gnash my teeth, and after about an hour of this my friend had presumably had enough of shouldering my grief alone and suggested we drop by Vicky's office.

Vicky was on duty that night, so had no escape, and for several hours she sat and listened to me cry and lament about the departure of my boyfriend. She offered many Kleenex and little advice. She didn't tell me (though it was quite true) that this boyfriend and I were never well suited to each other, that we had no future together, that I would get over him so totally that I would someday find it hard to believe I had ever dated him. Vicky could probably see all that (after all, she *was* 30, and a dean as well), but she didn't offer much commentary, just a listening ear. I do remember that once I apologized for something I had said, saying "But that's probably just a defense mechanism," and she said quickly: "Don't knock defense mechanisms. Do you know where we'd be without them? Defenseless!"

At some point during the evening—I don't recall what triggered it—Vicky suddenly began reciting Gerard Manley Hopkins' poem "Spring and Fall: To a Young Child." I was an English major; I had read the poem and loved it the previous semester in Victorian Literature. It was a short, though not simple, poem (none of Hopkins' poems are simple) about a little girl crying bitterly because the autumn leaves are falling from the trees. Though her sorrow is out of proportion to the occasion, the poem's speaker tells the girl that what she is really mourning for is the sorrow of the human condition: the death and loss we are all subject to. Later she will understand this; now she cries without really knowing why.

I don't think Vicky could have known that the poem was a favorite of mine, though she probably knew I had taken Victorian Lit. Perhaps it was a favorite of hers and she just assumed that as an English major I would be familiar with it. She recited it with no editorial comment and no elocutionary flourishes. In fact, she rattled it off extremely fast, almost auctioneer-pace, as if it were something she had memorized a long time ago and wanted to prove she could still do it. Maybe she just wanted to get the words out there and let them make their own point.

> *Margaret, are you grieving*
> *Over Goldengrove unleaving?*
> *Leaves, like the things of man, you*
> *With your fresh thoughts care for, can you?*
> *Ah! as the heart grows older*
> *It will come to such sights colder*
> *By and by, nor spare a sigh*
> *Though worlds of wanwood leafmeal lie;*
> *And yet you will weep and know why.*
> *Now no matter, child, the name:*
> *Sorrow's springs are the same.*
> *Nor mouth had, no nor mind, expressed*
> *What heart heard of, ghost guessed:*
> *It is the blight man was born for,*
> *It is Margaret you mourn for.*

I loved those lines—both their sound and their sense. I wasn't offended that Vicky equated my stormy grief with the child Margaret's naive heartbreak over the falling leaves. Even then I think I understood that my sorrow was out of proportion to the importance of the relationship, and I appreciated the implication that my grief, like Margaret's, was part of the universal sorrow for the human losses we all share.

Spring and Fall

I suspected then and am sure now that Vicky didn't greatly respect my boyfriend or my relationship with him—but she did respect my emotions and honor them, which I suppose was why I admired her so much.

My heart is older now, and colder, and I don't weep so intensely at life's losses. I sometimes remember Hopkins'(and Vicky's) words, though—when my toddler howls in anguish over some perceived injustice or a teenager in my youth group is depressed over a quarrel with a friend. *Now no matter, child, the name: Sorrow's springs are the same.* I don't want to belittle anyone's grief, for it springs out of the same well as mine did that night in Vicky's office: the hurt and pain and lostness of a worldful of people trying to make things work without God.

We're all in this together. Some of us are better at helping others get through it. Vicky was one of those. I'd like to be one too.

Rejoice with those who rejoice;
mourn with those who mourn.
Romans 12:15, NIV.

THINK IT THROUGH

1. Are you a "listener," or do you tend to get irritated or bored when people begin talking about their problems? If a friend comes to you with a need, are you more likely to encourage him or her to talk while you listen, or to start giving advice?

2. Who has listened sympathetically to you?

3. Is there anyone who needs you to listen to them right now?

35.

FIVE MINUTES MORE

This is a story about my dad and his guitar.

If you flip through the pages of this book, you'll find there's another story in here about my dad and his guitar—his beautiful 1953 Gibson Les Paul electric guitar.

This isn't about that guitar. This is about his first guitar, an acoustic guitar he owned a few years earlier, when he was about 14. He liked guitar music, thought the guitar might be a nice instrument to learn to play. He could pick out a couple chords here and there; he taught himself to string together a basic three-chord hurtin' song, but he wanted to learn to play really well—and for that, he had to find a teacher.

My dad—well, this was long before he was my dad, so I'll just call him Don—was at a friend's place, messing around on the guitar, showing off the few chords he did know, when a girl said, "I know a guy who's really good on the guitar. He could probably teach you to play, if you're looking for someone to give you lessons."

"Really?" Don said. "Who is he?" When the girl told him it was this guy Len, he got a little nervous. He knew the guy, a really good guitar player, but he didn't know him very well, and Len didn't seem like the kind of fellow who'd have a lot of time to waste on teenagers wanting to learn guitar.

But the girl said she'd ask, and later got back to him with the news that if he went by Len's place at 7:00 p.m. on Wednesday, he'd get a guitar lesson.

Five Minutes More

Don showed up, guitar in hand. The would-be guitar teacher didn't seem overly thrilled about giving him lessons, but he sat Don down and asked him what he could play, and Don played a couple pieces. Then Len pulled out a piece of sheet music, played through it, and showed Don the chords. It was a popular song called "Five Minutes More." When he'd finished playing it, Len handed it to Don and said, "Learn to play this song this week. Then come back same time next week and I'll give you a lesson, OK?"

The first lesson had lasted a total of about 10 minutes. But Don went home with his guitar in one hand and the sheet music to "Five Minutes More" in the other, and sat down that evening and started to learn it.

You probably don't know the song. I wouldn't, except that he played it now and then when I was growing up. My Web search tells me that Frank Sinatra sang it, though he may not have been the only one. It goes, "Five minutes more, only five minutes more, let me stay, let me stay, in your arms . . ."

Once Don got a good look at the music, he couldn't believe his eyes. He'd never even seen most of these chords—never mind being able to play them. And there were so many chord changes—it seemed like there was one for almost every word in the verse!

He stayed up late that night, figuring out the fingering, trying the chords. The next day he hurried home from school and picked up the guitar to try some more. All that week he worked away at that impossible song whenever he got a moment. It was the hardest thing he'd ever done, but by the time the next Wednesday evening came around, he could play every chord in it.

He got to Len's house at 7:00, so excited about his accomplishment and the upcoming lesson that he didn't notice the slight wrinkle of surprise on his teacher's forehead. "I can play it," he announced. "Well, it's kind of slow, but I can play it."

He sat down and cradled his guitar, singing along with the words as he made each difficult chord change. "Five . . . minutes . . . more . . . only . . . five . . . minutes . . . more."

It was painfully slow—possibly the only time "Five Minutes More" took more than five minutes to play. But he hit most of the chords, and when the song was done he looked up proudly.

"Not bad," said Len. "Now let's go over some of those chords . . ."

For the rest of that year Don got his weekly guitar lesson from Len. He was a fast learner, and he enjoyed every minute of it. And it wasn't till the lessons had gone on a long time that he finally had the nerve to ask why Len had given him such a tough piece to start off with—"Five Minutes More" wasn't exactly music for the beginning guitarist.

Len chuckled. "I hate giving lessons," he admitted. "Kids are always asking me for guitar lessons, and with most of them it's just a waste of time. So whenever anyone asks me for a lesson, I always give them that song and tell them to take it home and learn it before their next lesson." He paused. "Usually I never see them again. Sometimes they drop by to return the music and say they don't think they'll bother with the lessons. One guy actually mailed it back to me! But you're one of the few who ever learned it and came back for his lesson."

My dad has played guitar with tremendous skill and even greater love his whole life. And every chance he gets, he tells the story of Len and the song that was intended to separate the wheat from the chaff—to determine who really had the ability and, more important, the determination to learn to play.

You might not consider Len much of a mentor, except for his impressive guitar knowledge. He certainly didn't demonstrate unconditional love and acceptance, or an eagerness to mold young minds. But he did understand one important though unpopular fact: if you want to learn, if you want to succeed, it's going to take a lot more than five minutes.

**No one who puts his hand to the plow
and looks back is fit for service in the
kingdom of God. Luke 9:62, NIV.**

THINK IT THROUGH

1. Are you the type of person who's more likely to be motivated, or discouraged, by a really tough teacher or coach?

2. What's the hardest thing you've ever had to learn or study? Did anyone help you with it? Do you benefit more from a "hands-off" teacher like Len or a "hands-on" teacher who helps you more directly?

3. As a child, were you taught never to quit a hard task, or were you taught that it's OK to give up on things? How has that training affected the way you approach challenges in life?

36.

SUSAN AND THE SUBWAY

I started my first teaching job the same month I turned 21. The job was teaching high school in the province of Ontario, where the high school program at that time included one additional year beyond grade 12. So I was 21, teaching students as old as 19. In fact, there were two students in the school who had dropped out for a while and returned. They were both 22—a year older than I was.

To say this was a difficult assignment would be the understatement of the twentieth century (the century in which all this occurred). In retrospect I wish I had spent a year as a student missionary, spread out my college courses to take an extra year, or gone backpacking around Europe for 10 months—anything to have delayed the onset of adulthood for another year. When I stepped into my first classroom I simply was not ready for the job.

Anyone who's taught, even a little bit, knows that the first year of teaching is almost always overwhelming. When you're teaching large threatening people just a few years younger than yourself it's even more overwhelming. I was overwhelmed and almost sucked under. But, like most first-year teachers, I survived and lived to tell the story—and went on to teach for most of the next decade.

That first year the only people in my world more intimidating than the grade 12 and 13 students were the other teachers. Most of them were only in their mid-20s, a few years older than I, and hadn't been teaching much longer than I had. But to me they seemed

Susan and the Subway

mature, competent, and sensible beyond what I could ever hope to be. I was envious and terrified of them. Especially Susan.

Susan was my department head. Everyone in the school, even students, described her as the "perfect teacher." She maintained flawless discipline in all her classes. Every student I ever talked to both respected and liked her. Other teachers looked up to her. The administration loved her; she was perfectly organized, always prompt, and would never dream of turning in her grades two days late (something I tried during the first grading period I ever lived through).

You know, in a lot of places in this book I've changed and rearranged details to protect people's identities, but the above paragraph isn't one of them. Only Susan's name is changed. I know it's difficult to believe anyone could be such a paragon, but she really was. Oh, and she was a genuinely nice person—sweet, likable, self-effacing, humble. You couldn't even have the satisfaction of hating her for being so perfect.

I admired Susan. I didn't exactly want to be like her, because I knew I never could, but I wanted to be in her league. I didn't want to look like an incompetent, bumbling idiot anytime I stood next to her. But that was how I felt.

I taught at that school for four years, and eventually Susan and I became friends. Never best friends, but we enjoyed being together, and I could talk to her without feeling like the geeky girl talking to the cool girl. Once I even had the nerve to tell her I wished she'd given me more guidance, more direction, during my confusing and scary first year of teaching. "I would have," she replied, "but I didn't know you needed it. I had no idea you needed help." I wish now I had asked. But asking for help isn't that easy.

The change in our relationship occurred somewhat naturally, as I got older and grew in confidence. But one incident made a big difference.

At the beginning of my third year teaching, Susan and I were scheduled to attend a series of workshops together in the big city of Toronto, about an hour from campus. I loved Toronto. It was the biggest city I'd ever lived near, and on the weekends or in the evenings I liked taking the Go-Train to a play or concert or to shop at the Eaton Centre. The one thing I didn't like was driving on the crowded, busy city streets, so I used the public transit system. I loved the subways, loved memorizing the names of the stops and figuring out the best route to my destination. I've always been a big fan of maps and transit systems, so finding my way around Toronto came naturally to me.

The day before our workshop Susan and I were figuring out how we'd get into downtown Toronto by 9:00 the next morning for our meetings. Like me, she didn't like the idea of driving downtown, and it would take forever in rush-hour traffic anyway.

"Couldn't your husband drive us to the Go-Station, so we could take the train in?" I asked.

"Sure, but that only goes to Scarborough; how would we get downtown from there?"

I looked as Susan as though she'd forgotten her own name. "On the subway."

She looked at me as though I'd suggested snake handling for a class assignment. "The subway? I've never been on the subway. I'm a little scared of it."

"You what?" I was completely floored. Susan had grown up in the suburbs of Toronto. She had lived there all her life—and she had never been on the subway? What's more, she was *scared* of it? I literally couldn't believe what I was hearing.

"Susan, the subway's nothing to be scared of. I take it all the time."

"Then you'd know how to get from Scarborough to where the workshop is?"

"Well, yeah—I mean, it's a direct line. You get on, you ride for a half hour, you get off and walk one block."

"OK, well, you'll just have to lead the way tomorrow."

And I did. Bravely I led Susan onto the first subway ride of her 28 years. I, the small-town girl from Newfoundland, steered her competently through the token booth, up and down the escalators, onto and off of subway cars. Susan was impressed. I was elated. I had finally found something I was better at than she was!

Now that I've written it down, this looks very petty. And partly it was. I just wanted to excel in something, to stop feeling so inferior to Susan all the time. I needed a tiny little victory, and I got it.

Susan and the Subway

But from another angle, it makes sense. Everyone's good at something. OK, so Susan was good at something important, like her chosen life career, while I was merely good at finding my away around public transit. But still, we each excelled in some area. I needed to see Susan as a human being with weaknesses as well as strengths—and I needed to see myself as strong too.

I owe a lot to Susan. Even though I didn't always directly ask her for the help I needed, I followed her example a lot as I grew into a teacher. She became a true mentor, one I'll always be grateful to. But I don't think I'd ever have had the courage to come closer if I hadn't seen a tiny weak spot in her armor.

> **The entire law is summed up in a
> single command: "Love your neighbor
> as yourself." (Galatians 5:14, NIV.)**

THINK IT THROUGH

1. Many people interpret the command "Love your neighbor as yourself" to imply that God wants us to love ourselves before we can properly love our neighbors. Do you agree with this? Why or why not?

2. How have you found that your self-esteem affects the way you view and treat other people? Do you need to feel good about yourself in order to feel good toward other people?

37.

THE TOUGHEST QUESTION

I was hit with some difficult questions during the 11 years I spent teaching high school English and history. Many of these actually related to my subject area. The first time it happened, I was teaching the play *Macbeth* to a grade 12 class. I was standing with my back to the class, writing notes on the board and explaining them at the same time, when a student said, "The review questions said something about sleep imagery in the play. What does that mean?"

The only problem with this question was that I had no idea what the answer was. I hadn't studied *Macbeth* myself in college, had read it over only once, to prepare for this course. I didn't have the faintest clue whether there was any sleep imagery in the play—or what it meant.

To my amazement, I discovered I was talking. "Well, Joel, you see, when we talk about imagery in one of Shakespeare's plays . . ." I realized that if I dragged out what I was saying long enough, I would give myself time to think. Under the tremendous adrenaline pressure of my entire class staring at me and learning I was a complete idiot, my mind flew. Thoughts dropped into place seconds before they left my lips. In two minutes I had given Joel a complete and thorough answer on the subject of sleep imagery in *Macbeth,* and the beauty of it was—*I had made it up as I went along!*

The Toughest Question

This was a turning point in my teaching. I realized that you don't actually have to know what you're talking about in order to teach. You just have to be able to think on your feet. OK, a rudimentary knowledge of the subject matter is essential—I couldn't pull this trick off if I were teaching Fundamentals of Calculus. But you don't have to know the answer to the exact question you're being asked. You just have to sound like you do.

I used this little skill (which, by the way, you won't find recommended in any of your textbooks if you're studying education, but I assure you that every teacher out there knows and uses, because saying "I don't know" to a classful of teenagers is like going among wolves with a "Please Eat Me, I'm a Sheep" sign on your back) frequently over the next few years. I discovered I could make up answers plausible enough to cover until I had time to look up the real answer—which I could then present as "extra research material."

This amazing ability to spout spontaneous nonsense did me no good whatever, though, when I finally faced one of the few *real* questions I've ever been asked.

This one, of course, had nothing to do with English literature (sadly, very few of life's real questions ever do). And of course Ashley should have saved the question for her Bible teacher, but the problem was, she was thinking about the question there and then, in English class, so I was the teacher available. And just as my students assumed that any English teacher should be able to answer any question about Shakespeare or poetry or grammar, they also assumed that any Christian teacher in any Christian school should probably be able to handle a question about faith or God or eternity.

Ashley wasn't from the same church background as I was, but she had attended our Seventh-day Adventist school very happily and successfully for two years. She was from a single-parent family in kind of a rough area of town, but she was a good kid who worked hard at being a good student. She was in grade 8 when I first taught her, and in grade 10 when her father died.

The thing is, we didn't know at first it was Ashley's father. All the news told us was that Steve Mackenzie had been shot dead in a downtown parking lot, and that his brother Dave Mackenzie was the suspect. The name Mackenzie was infamous in our town. One brother, Rob Mackenzie, was already in jail for murdering a woman a few years before, and the rest of the family was split between those who believed Rob was innocent and those who thought he was guilty. Given the Mackenzie record of drug dealing, violence, and crime, a family feud was likely to be a feud in the truest sense.

So most of us just shook our heads in a "What would you expect?" kind of way when we heard that one Mackenzie brother had shot and killed another. And that was all I thought of it until next morning in staff meeting, when our principal said, "Did you know that Steve Mackenzie was Ashley Brown's father?"

We were all shocked. Suddenly what had been a tasty tidbit of news gossip had become real and close to home. We learned that Ashley had never lived with her father—he and her mother had never been married, and had gone their separate ways years ago—but that she had been in contact with him and his family, that she sometimes visited him.

Ashley didn't appear in school for several days after her father's death. When she did come back, I thought she would be embarrassed to talk about her dad's death and the circumstances of it, but she showed a true Mackenzie fighting spirit and was willing to take on the subject with anyone. In my speech class she wanted to do her argumentative speech about "Why My Uncle Dave Should Be Found Guilty of My Dad's Murder," with her grandmother as her main source material.

It was kind of tragic and kind of surreal. Almost funny, to someone safely removed from it. Then Ashley hit me with the question. She and her friend Nina had been whispering in the back of class all through their study time. I'd told them a couple times to be quiet, but it was obvious whatever they were discussing was far more fascinating than their English assignment.

Then, as they were leaving class, both girls stopped at my desk, and Ashley said, "Miss, I've got a question for you. Will my dad be in heaven?"

Well, now. That was one they hadn't prepared me for in Secondary Methods class.

The Toughest Question

Fortunately Ashley was a big talker, so she went on before I had to come up with a reply. "'Cause you see, Miss, he did do a lot of bad things, like he was into drugs and he did stuff that was against the law and stuff, but then he was a really sweet person too—he was really good and kind and sweet, and he used to pray. He told me he prayed to God every night, so I know he believed in God. So will he go to heaven?"

And there I was, with all those years of experience making up answers on the spot finally coming to my aid. I opened my mouth and words came out.

"Well, Ashley, only God knows a person's heart. Other people judged your dad by the things they saw, but only God knew what he was really like inside. That's what God judges by—what a person is like inside. We can trust God to do what's best for your dad."

That seemed to satisfy her. We didn't talk any more about it. She said, "OK, thanks," and left the room. And she never brought it up again.

And I was left to wonder: Was the answer I made up off the top of my head good enough? It did happen to be what I really believed. Was I more concerned about looking like I knew all the answers than about really connecting with Ashley? In three years of teaching her, I had one moment to really touch her life, to talk with her about something eternal, something that mattered. One moment more than I've had with a lot of students.

I know You sent me that moment, God. And I'm still praying I didn't mess it up.

There is only one Lawgiver and Judge, the one who is able to save and destroy. But you—who are you to judge your neighbor? James 4:12, NIV.

THINK IT THROUGH

1. How would you have answered Ashley's question?

2. What's the toughest question anyone has ever asked you? Did you feel prepared to answer it?

LOVE AND ROMANCE

Sometimes it seems as if your young adult years are about only one thing—looking for someone to fall in love with and marry.

Sorry, that's probably too sweeping and general. Let me rephrase that: it seemed like only one thing was truly important in my life between the ages of 18 and 30 (I got married when I was 30)—looking for someone to fall in love with and marry. Yes, I got two college degrees and launched a career in there somewhere, lived in three different Canadian provinces and one U.S. state, even wrote eight books—but all that was peripheral. My life was really about whom I was or wasn't in love with, how the relationship or the search was progressing, and whether I was going to get married.

I don't think I'm unique in this. For both males and females, this quest takes up an incredible amount of time and energy during most of the 20s (unless you get married at 19, in which case you probably spend your 20s figuring out how this marriage thing works). I recall learning in a college psychology class that one of the major life tasks during the young adult years was "finding a love object." I loved the detached, clinical sound of that phrase. Yes, if I could just walk into the Love Shop and pick the right Love Object off the shelf, I'd be set for life.

Eventually I found my Love Object (read all about it in chapter 40), but both the search and the discovery proved to be a gold mine of self-discovery and spiritual training. God's ideal for every person who chooses to marry (not everyone does, or should) is that spouses should reflect God's unconditional, perfect love to each other. We don't often get it right, at least not to that extent, but it's wonderful when we do. As for the times we get it wrong—well, those are opportunities to grow and learn.

When I started asking people for story ideas for this book, I got more in the category of "Love and Marriage" than any other—which confirmed my suspicion that this is a pretty major obsession for most of us. Some were tales of love gone wrong; some were tales of love gone beautifully and emphatically right. Each was a portrait of how God reaches through our tangled web of relationships and shows us Himself in the middle of it all.

38.

HOW I GOT FLEECED

I walked through the double doors at the back of the chapel. I had come down to worship alone, so I paused for that inevitable moment of decision: where to sit? whom to sit with? Tuesday night was joint worship—guys and girls together in the girls' dorm chapel—so there was a little more risk involved in the choice than there would normally be.

A cluster of my friends sat near the front on the left side, and I was just about to join them when I saw Edwin.

Edwin sat alone, in the middle on the right-hand side of the chapel. Every nerve in my body strained in the opposite direction. I did *not* want to sit with Edwin.

Not that Edwin was a bad person. His worst crime was that he bored me—which, I guess, meant nothing worse than that he and I weren't interested in the same things. He'd asked me out three times, and twice I'd actually said yes. Two dates, I figured, was giving anyone a fair shot. Two dates, plus several lunches in the cafeteria, were more than enough for me to realize that Edwin and I had absolutely nothing in common. Finding things to talk about was a strain.

Unfortunately, this was one of those sad times when the feeling wasn't mutual. I didn't think we had anything in common, but Edwin obviously thought we did. He kept sitting with me at lunch, calling me, trying to arrange dates that I politely tried to avoid.

But as I saw him alone in the chapel, I felt sorry for him. He didn't have a whole lot of close friends. I wasn't the only girl he had asked out repeatedly—he was really looking for a girlfriend, looking for someone to care about him. He wasn't stupid or ugly or obnoxious or anything—he just hadn't found Ms. Right yet. And here he was, sitting all alone at joint worship in the girls' dorm chapel.

So I decided to do the kind thing, the Christian thing. I would sit beside Edwin. It wasn't as if sitting together in worship required us to talk a lot.

It wasn't that bad. He smiled as I sat down, and we had a short whispered how-was-your-day kind of conversation as song service started. Then we sat back and listened to the program. Afterward we exchanged a few more banal comments and said good night. Simple and painless, and I'd brought a little sunshine to this lonely boy's day.

Then the phone rang.

It was about an hour after worship, and I was back in my room studying. I picked up the phone, said hi, and felt my stomach knot as I heard Edwin's voice. Hadn't I already discharged my duty to him?

"Hi, Trudy."

"Uh, hi, Edwin."

"It was real nice of you to come sit with me at worship tonight."

"Oh, well—no big deal, thanks."

"No, I was really glad you did."

"Oh, OK."

"Wanna know why I was so glad?"

Obviously the honest answer to this was that I did not want to know, but instead I said, "Why?"

"Because before I went to worship tonight, I prayed."

"You did?" The knot got tighter.

"Yep. And you know what I asked God?"

"No." I didn't, although I was dreading the answer.

"I asked Him for a sign that you and me were meant to be to-gether. I asked Him for you to come and sit with me in worship tonight, and if you did, that would be a sign that we were meant to be together."

How I Got Fleeced

Silence. *Loooonnnggg* silence. This was going to be a very, very difficult conversation.

"Well, Edwin, um, I mean, I'm not sure God works that way, you know, all the time . . ."

You have to realize that Edwin and I had already had the "Let's just be friends" talk. I had made it as clear as humanly possible that this relationship was not happening. Now here I was trying to explain my philosophy of how we can know God's will to a guy who thought I was the answer to his prayers.

Ever since Gideon put out that fleece in the Old Testament, people have been asking God for signs. The problem was, I wasn't going to be Edwin's fleece. I was (and am) a real human being, capable of making my own choices and decisions.

The fact is, though, that I'm as much a sucker for signs as the next Christian. In fact, when I was 7 years old and had been deeply impacted by the story of Gideon, I asked God for a sign that He really existed. I laid my red plush Squirmin' Hermin out at the foot of my bed and prayed that God would make it turn yellow by morning.

I still have my Squirmin' Hermin—what's left of it, as the cat got at it a few years ago and pulled it to pieces with her claws and teeth. The pieces are still bravely, defiantly red. I don't know how I explained God's failure to my 7-year-old self. Probably about as smoothly as I explained it to Edwin on the phone that night.

If it worked once, for Gideon, why doesn't it always work for us today? I think most of us like the idea of signs. We want a simple answer, something we can point to and say, "There! That's God's will!" Unfortunately, we don't get many of those.

I didn't want to be Edwin's fleece, yet sometimes I envy his simple faith. Finding God's will for our lives isn't always easy, and one of the most difficult parts of that quest is finding the person you're going to share your life with. Many times in my single years I wanted God to light a giant neon arrow over the head of some guy in the cafeteria, with flashing letters that spelled out "HE'S THE ONE!"

Most of us don't get that. I didn't. Edwin didn't. Instead, we have a lot of other tools to know God's will—His Word, the advice of mature Christians, our own reason, His providential leading. We spend a lifetime learning to add all those things up and come up with a map of what God wants for our lives.

In fact, finding God's will for our lives isn't really much like following a road map. It's a dialogue, a relationship between God and us—perhaps more like talking to God on your car phone while He gives you directions to His house. "OK, you're at the lights . . . now turn left . . . you can take a right now . . . I see you at the top of the street . . . this is My driveway, I'm standing out on the step waving to you. Hey, you're here! Welcome home."

I don't know where Edwin is or what he's doing now. I hope he's learned that there are better (though harder) ways to know God's will than asking for a sign—especially a sign that hinges on someone else's free will. I certainly hope he's found Ms. Right and is as happily married as I am. Most of all, I guess, I hope he's still talking to God, still searching, as I am, for God's directions on the road.

**"I know the plans I have for you,"
declares the Lord, "plans to prosper you
and not to harm you, plans to give you
hope and a future." Jeremiah 29:11, NIV.**

THINK IT THROUGH

1. Is there one "Mr. Right" or "Ms. Right" for everyone? If so, how can we be sure we've found that person?

2. Have you ever asked God for a sign? Did you get your sign? How did it impact your decision?

3. How do you search for God's will in your life?

39.

LEAST VALUABLE PLAYER

Saturday night on an Adventist college campus. A vast assortment of entertainment options lay spread before the students. Well, maybe not that vast—but there were a few choices. The main event of the evening, though, was a movie in the gym.

Larry and Donna decided to take in the movie. They had just reached the stage of dating at which they assumed they'd be doing something together Saturday night without necessarily having to "ask" each other out. It was a delicate balance—they were getting comfortable with each other, but not comfortable enough to presume too much. When Larry said, "What were you thinking about doing Saturday night?" and Donna said, "Maybe we could go to that movie they're showing in the gym," Larry felt a little rush of relief at the realization that she too was making plans for them to be together.

So Saturday night came, and they agreed over the phone to meet at the student center at 7:00. Larry dropped by a friend's place off-campus for a quick supper. It was winter; the sun had already set; Larry's friend had the television on.

"Hey, there's a hockey game on," one of the guys said.

The TV drew Larry's attention like a magnet. A transplanted Canadian in the U.S., he was an avid hockey fan and watched NHL games whenever he got a chance. He'd been standing up eating Mr. Noodles from a Styrofoam cup, but when he saw the game in progress he lowered himself onto the couch. It was 6:30 p.m.

CONNECTING

Soon Larry and his friends were all cheering enthusiastically as the players flew past on the ice. The first period ended scoreless, and during the intermission Larry got involved in a heated argument with one of his friends about how this team had recently traded their goalie and whether that had been a good move or a bad one.

Just seconds into the second period the home team scored, but the other team quickly tied it. Larry remained riveted to the screen as the minutes flew past. The second period ended with a score of 2-1.

"Well, I hate to leave," one of the guys said, standing and stretching, "but I've got a date. See you all later."

The words echoed in the frozen arena of Larry's brain like a sudden-death buzzer. *I've got a date . . . got a date . . . got a date . . .*

He automatically turned over his wrist to check his watch, yet he could hardly drag his eyes down to look. *No, please, don't let it be—*

It was 8:00 p.m.

"Guys, I'm in big trouble," Larry announced, leaping from the couch and pulling on his jacket.

He ran out the door and up the road toward campus. When he was within sight of the gym, he paused. Where to look? Surely Donna would have gone ahead to the movie. She'd probably be sitting with some of her friends, enjoying the show. He hoped she was enjoying the movie enough that she wouldn't want to do anything to ruin it, such as murder him in the middle of it.

How could he have been so stupid? Sure, the hockey game was interesting, fascinating even. It certainly had seemed important at the time—important enough that he didn't even notice the hours passing. Important enough to make him forget everything else. But was it as important as Donna? A lousy hockey game? How could it even compare?

The gym was dark. The air smelled of warm bodies and popcorn. In the glow from the big screen Larry edged down the aisles, scanning faces. Finally he saw a group of Donna's friends, but she wasn't with them. After two more trips up and down the aisles, he had to admit: She wasn't there.

Which meant he'd made a very bad miscalculation. He'd wasted time looking for her in the wrong place, and now he was *even later than he had been.*

Least Valuable Player

Should he go to her dorm? Would she be in her room, pacing the floor, throwing things? Or was she off campus altogether, gone out with friends to forget the whole thing—or worse yet, gone out with another guy?

Just before he finally drove himself insane considering all the possibilities, Larry decided to check out the student center. He ran up the steps and quickly scanned the lounge. Except for one couple playing chess together in the corner, it was empty. He turned to go.

"Fancy meeting you here," said a voice from a nearby couch.

She was partially hidden behind a potted plant. She stood up, gazing at him evenly. Her eyes were like ice. Sort of like that stuff hockey players skate on.

"Donna, I'm so sorry, I can explain, it was really stupid, I'm so sorry . . ." Larry's words tumbled over themselves. He was babbling, repeating himself, all but kneeling on the floor at her feet in his eagerness to apologize.

It took quite a bit of apology. Donna was madder than he'd ever realized a woman could be. She had some very well chosen words to say about his choices, and what they revealed about his priorities—and there were a few comments on thoughtlessness in there, and the word "stupidity" even crept into the conversation. She was very thorough, coherent, and well organized—compared to Larry, who sounded like a raving lunatic. But then she'd had an hour and a half to rehearse everything she wanted to say, while he was working off the top of his head.

Well, Donna had a point there, didn't she? Apart from being careless, thoughtless, and forgetful, wasn't Larry actually revealing that he cared more about watching a hockey game than about going out with her? Didn't this man have his priorities severely out of line?

It's a fascinating study to compare and contrast the things we say are important to us with the things we actually *choose* to spend our time on. If you agree to the proposition that how you spend your time is the truest measure of your priorities, what would be the most important thing in your life?

Many people say that family comes first—yet they spend 50 or 60 hours a week at work, leaving their families with only a few left-over hours. Lots of students claim their top priority is making good grades, yet study time is relegated to a few odd hours in between social engagements. Most of us say, if we're Christians, that we want to put God first in our lives, yet our weekly time with Him barely adds up to the length of one TV sitcom.

Larry would have said that his relationship with Donna came first in his life. Certainly ahead of any lousy hockey game. But his choices revealed something different.

You'll be glad to know that this story has a happy ending. Donna forgave Larry. They kept dating. They married and now have three lovely children. Larry still enjoys hockey games, but he also (usually) remembers appointments he's made with his wife—although, he says, relating this story from the safe distance of several years, "She still reminds me of that story every once in a while."

I'll bet she does. Wouldn't you?

**You shall have no other
gods before me. Exodus 20:3, NIV.**

THINK IT THROUGH

1. Are your priorities in balance with the way you actually choose to spend your time? If not, what does your use of time reveal?

2. If you really put God first in your life, how would your everyday choices be different?

40.

THE PLASTIC BAG

Some people are romantics. For these people, the symbol of undying love might be a perfect red rose, a golden chain, a flawless diamond. If two romantics marry, they may cherish forever the memory of "their song," the piece of music whose lyrics and melody perfectly embody their undying love. They may visit over and over the quaint Victorian garden where their hearts first entwined as one, or that little sidewalk café where a mutual glance told them they each felt the same.

I'm not a romantic. For me, the eternal symbol of my husband's love for me, the one defining thing that made me sure he was "the one," is a plastic grocery-store bag filled with—well, with something quite unromantic.

The circumstances were not at all conducive to romance. True, we were in Quebec City, the old city, one of the most beautiful and historic sites in North America. But we weren't alone there. We were accompanied by 37 Pathfinders, and I'll defy anyone to try to find romance blossoming on a Pathfinder Camporee—at least among the leaders.

Several days before the memorable incident we had left our homes in St. John's, Newfoundland, on a yellow school bus filled with Pathfinders and a few other Pathfinder counselors like ourselves. The 37 kids seemed blessed with boundless energy. When they were happy, well rested, and well fed they screamed, shouted, sang "We are soldiers in the army" over and over and over, and bounced around the bus like peas in a tin can. When they were cranky, hungry, and tired, they fought, whined, screamed, shouted, and bounced around the bus like peas in a tin can. The bus seats were so hard they could have been carved from marble. We stopped for bathroom visits every 2.5 miles, except when I needed to go, in which case we drove on for hours without pausing.

We were on our way to camp at Val d'Espoir, Quebec (a four-day drive from home). Val d'Espoir means "Valley of Hope," I think, but you can pronounce it "Val Despair" if you want, and since the Quebec Conference has since sold the place I'll be straight about this and say that was the best way to pronounce it. As a campsite it was entirely without redeeming features—there was no lake, no hills, few trees, nothing scenic or picturesque. Showers were inside and warmish on odd days, outside and freezing cold on even days. The weather was hot, hot, hot, and we and our Pathfinders were quartered in old-fashioned canvas tents that trapped the heat and seemed to shut out any breath of fresh air that might trickle by. Oh, there was a swimming pool, but something green was floating on the surface.

With all this, plus having to control a bunch of 9- and 10-year-olds, you might think this wasn't my dream vacation, but you'd be oh, so wrong. Because my boyfriend was along, and we were sharing this wonderful adventure together, and at least we had each other to complain to.

The day I looked forward to most all week was Wednesday, the day we were scheduled to visit Quebec City. I had traveled widely around Canada but had never been to this historic city, and despite the fact that we would have a crew of Pathfinders trailing after us, Jason and I looked forward to seeing the old buildings, shopping at quaint little markets and boutiques, and holding hands as we strolled down the cobblestone streets.

On Wednesday morning I woke up feeling sick to my stomach. Since I was still in the canvas tent, I didn't think much of this, but assumed I'd feel better as soon as I got outside and started breathing. But after breakfast I still felt queasy, which was unusual. (You might

The Plastic Bag

think I'm about to complain about the food at this point, but in fact the food was delicious. The cooks, at least, got full marks from me.) When I had to run to the outdoor bathrooms (the less said about those the better) to throw up, I knew this was not going to be the day I'd dreamed of.

The sensible choice would have been to stay back at the camp. But I just couldn't face that thought. A day all alone, lying on the ground inside the horrible canvas tent while the temperature climbed outside, far away from Jason and never, ever getting to see Quebec City—and for all I knew, I might be feeling better by lunchtime and kicking myself for not making the trip. I told our Pathfinder director I was going to go anyway, and she gave me a plastic grocery bag to hold in case I needed to throw up while on the bus ride.

I didn't. My stomach didn't entirely settle down, but I no longer felt an imminent urge to vomit, though I kept a tight grip on the plastic bag. My spirits lifted a little. This was really going to be OK.

We finally pulled into a parking lot in the city and got out, ready to hit the walking trail that circles the walls of the old city. Cameras and guidebooks in hand, we piled off the bus and began collecting stray Pathfinders.

I was walking across the grass when it hit—the need to use my plastic bag. At once. I had no time to look for a washroom. I just went behind a tree and—well, I'll be sensitive. Let's just say that I looked up from my plastic bag, feeling utterly miserable, my face sweaty, my hair sticking to my cheeks—and whom should I see but Jason, my boyfriend, hovering nearby. He came up and put an arm around me. "How are you doing?" he asked gently.

Then he did the amazing thing. He took the plastic bag, with its unpleasant cargo, from my hand, tied it shut, and said, "I'll take care of that. You just wait right here."

I watched in amazement as this man I had dated for less than a year walked across the green grass of Quebec City and deposited a plastic bag full of my—well, you know—in a garbage can. Then he came back and said, "Do you feel well enough to go on the walk?"

I did—marginally. You know the level of sick when you feel

sort of almost-all-right in between throw-ups? That was the kind of afternoon I was having. We did see a little of the old city, and we took some pictures of us together and us with our Pathfinders. I had two more plastic-bag incidents—in both cases Jason found me a bag, stood by me while I filled it, and then disposed of it. After the third time I didn't feel well enough to go on, and Jason got directions to take me to the nearest public washroom, which happened to be in the lobby of the fabulously luxurious (and air-conditioned!) Chateau Frontenac Hotel.

I have to say that the Chateau Frontenac is by far the classiest place I have ever been sick—and I managed to make it to the bathroom there too. I insisted that Jason go on with the others, so at least one of us could enjoy Quebec City, and once I'd had a nice trip to the clean, cool, marble-walled washroom I curled up on a soft velvety couch in that lovely air-conditioned lobby, and started to feel a lot better, and actually drifted off to sleep. Nobody came to kick me out, which was nice, and a couple hours later Jason returned with a small souvenir pin of the Chateau Frontenac, so I'd always remember my visit. I think I would have anyway.

So I don't have a lot of memories of historic Quebec City, but I do have a husband, whom I married a few years later. I told this story at our wedding—not a very romantic thing to do, perhaps, but I had to make the point that there are some things more important than romance. Jason is a bit of a romantic, and over the years he has sent me roses several times, and bought me lovely cards and gifts and taken me to dinner. But none of those things has made as much impression as the sight of him on that hot day in Quebec City, walking to the garbage can with that plastic bag.

I thought at that moment: *Here's a guy who'll stick by me. Here's someone who's not afraid of the ugly, rough, and difficult parts of life. Here's a guy who'll coach me through labor and delivery, who'll change the baby's diapers, who'll be around when I'm sick or scared or miserable, who'll clean the cat's litter box and pick the gucky stuff out of the sink strainer. Those are the important things. Roses will fade and even diamonds lose their shine, but the guy who'll carry the plastic bag—that's the guy you want around.*

The Plastic Bag

Ten years have passed since our trip to Quebec City, and you know what? I was right on every count.

**Husbands, love your wives, just as
Christ loved the church and gave
himself up for her. Ephesians 5:25, NIV.**

THINK IT THROUGH

1. What's the most romantic thing someone has ever done for you? What's the most self-sacrificing thing someone you dated has ever done for you? Which matters more to you?

2. What's the most self-sacrificing thing you've ever done for another person?

3. Have you ever seen a reflection of God's unconditional love in the love of another human being? When, where, and how?

41.

LONG DISTANCE

I guess most of us have had a long-distance relationship at some point. I've fallen victim to them many times. But I was never quite so far from my beloved as my friend Lori was from Karl.

Lori met Karl in college. He was spending a year studying in the U.S., and they quickly discovered how much they had in common and started dating. They had a good time—until the school year ended and he headed home to Germany.

It would have been easier, maybe, just to break up. Instead they agreed they would keep in touch, see where the relationship led. She planned to come visit at Christmas. Perhaps he would be back in the States next summer.

This was in ancient times, before the invention of e-mail. Each week Lori faithfully sat down, picked up a real ballpoint pen, and wrote an actual letter on paper. Then she folded it, put it in an envelope, brought it to the mailbox, and waited for it to make its agonizingly slow journey across the seas to Europe. (It really is hard to remember we once did this.)

Each week Karl's letters came in return. Lori unfolded them to read about Karl's classes, the hard day he'd had at his job, his family, what he and his friends did on Saturday night. The little jokes and affectionate words sprinkled throughout each letter made it seem, for a moment, as if they were in the same room.

Sabbath was the best day of Lori's week, because she and Karl

Long Distance

had an agreement to phone each other every Sabbath. When it was her turn to call she punched the long international number with trembling fingers, eager to hear his voice again. When it was his week, she jumped with anticipation every time the phone rang. Then, for a few too-short minutes, she could actually hear his voice, laugh with him, imagine she was sitting beside him.

Christmas came, and Lori went to Germany. Hand in hand she strolled with him down the streets of his hometown, hearing the stories of his childhood and his teenage years. They kissed by the mailbox where he mailed her weekly letters. They shopped for European souvenirs for Lori to bring home as Christmas gifts for her friends and family.

In the weeks after the visit their letters were thick and their phone calls were long, full of memories of the visit and plans for the summer. Yes, Karl was definitely going to come over. They would spend the summer together, and then . . . well, they'd just have to see what happened.

But as February shivered its way into March, something changed. One week Lori faithfully posted her letter as usual, but no letter from Karl arrived that week. When he called on Sabbath he told her how busy he was, so she didn't mention the letter. She wrote again the next week, but again there was no letter from Karl. A card arrived the next week with just a few lines scribbled next to a cartoon picture. The printed message said he missed her, but his own casual signature made her wonder.

One Sabbath in March it was Karl's turn to call. Lori ran for the phone when it rang at the usual time after church, but it was a friend asking her to come over for a while. She waited a little longer, but there was no call. Finally she went to her friend's house for a few hours. Then, as the evening wore on with no phone call from Karl, she convinced herself he must have called while she was out.

But he didn't call back on Saturday night or on Sunday. She wanted to call him, to find out why, but she didn't want him to feel crowded or smothered. Surely he would call during the week.

She called him the next Sabbath, since it was her turn. The conversation was a little strained. He apologized for not calling the week before. He'd gone away for the day with some friends, and then it had been a really busy week, and . . .

She hung up feeling cold inside. She couldn't imagine a week so busy she wouldn't want to talk to Karl.

Another week went by, then two. No more letters. No Sabbath phone call. Lori knew what was happening, yet she couldn't accept it. She kept sending short cheerful notes and cards. She no longer felt like writing long letters. She just wanted to hear Karl's voice, even to see his handwriting, to be assured that he still cared and he was still thinking about her. But the silence grew and widened, as long as the miles between them.

Lori isn't married to Karl. He really did stop writing and calling because he wasn't interested anymore. Some people have heartwarming success stories about their long-distance relationships, but for most of us, absence really does make the heart go wander. It's hard to keep love alive when days and weeks go by with no communication.

In those long days and weeks waiting for the phone to ring, for a letter to arrive, Lori caught a little glimpse of how God must feel. He's invested everything He has—holding nothing back, not playing it safe—in the ultimate long-distance relationship. He's given all He has to a bunch of people He loves passionately—people who live so far away they can't see Him or hear Him speak.

How His heart must jump every time the "prayer phone" rings! He wants to hear your voice—to know that you still care, that you still want to keep in touch, that you're not drifting apart from Him. How does He feel when day after day slips by, and the appointment that used to be so special—your time with Him—is forgotten in the busyness of daily life?

Most long-distance relationships don't make it. Most of ours, and most of God's. I want my long-distance love affair with God to be one of the success stories. And I know what it takes—why is it sometimes so hard to pick up that phone?

In my Father's house are many rooms; if it were not so, I would have told you. I am going there

**to prepare a place for you. And if I go and
prepare a place for you, I will come back and
take you to be with me that you also may be
where I am. John 14: 2, 3, NIV.**

**Pray continually.
1 Thessalonians 5:17, NIV.**

THINK IT THROUGH

1. When was the last time you made meaningful contact with God? If He was a human long-distance lover, would He be satisfied with the amount of communication He has with you?

2. Is it difficult for you to think of God as a lover, an intimate friend? If so, how can you make His love for you more real, more relevant to your everyday life?

42.

"YOU HAVE TO CHOOSE"

When Danielle was 19 she met Dave. They had a lot in common; they had a lot of fun together. In fact, the only big difference between them was that Danielle was a Christian, active in her church, and Dave had no interest in any kind of religion.

At first it didn't matter much. They went to ball games together and went out for pizza afterward. They went for long walks on warm summer evenings. They laughed and talked and avoided any subject that would make either of them uncomfortable. There were plenty of other things to talk about and think about.

But Danielle kept going to church on Sabbath, continued to be involved in her youth group. She invited Dave to come out to youth meetings with her, even to social activities with friends from church, but he never wanted to come. He made it pretty clear that that was a part of her life he wanted nothing to do with.

And so it got more difficult. There were more times he wanted to go out and she had other plans. Dave began to get irritated about the Sabbath. Why couldn't Danielle go to the mall or to a game on Saturday? Why did she have to be such a fanatic?

She tried to explain. He told her to stop preaching at him.

One evening Danielle went to a service at church. It was a good program—good music, an inspiring speaker. She had asked Dave to come, but he wanted to do something else. She really wanted to go to this particular meeting, so they'd agreed to go their separate ways that evening. It was too bad, but on her way home Danielle felt so good, so positive, that even a disagreement with Dave couldn't dampen her spirit. She was uplifted, encouraged, close to God.

Dave was sitting on her front step.

She got out of the car and slowly walked toward him. "How was your church thing?" he asked. He sounded pretty relaxed, and the knot of tension that had been inside without her even knowing it loosened a little.

"It was OK. It was great, actually. I had a great time."

"Yeah, well, I didn't. I wanted to be with you."

"You could have come with me," Danielle said, sitting slowly down on the step beside him. The knot tightened again.

"Not like that. That's not what I mean. I wanted you to be out with me—not at your stupid church."

They talked for a long time—long past midnight, sitting there on the steps, trying to untangle something that was never meant to be straightened out. They had so much in common, yet there was no common ground. No room for a compromise.

Just before he left, Dave said something that shocked Danielle. "You're going to have to make a choice, Dani," he said. "You're going to have to choose between me and your God."

Danielle said nothing. There was nothing to say. Dave went home. He didn't mention seeing her tomorrow or calling later.

When he had gone Danielle stood alone at her bedroom window, looking out at the stars, achingly clear in the midnight sky. Tears ran down her cheeks. *Why, Lord?* she asked silently. *All I wanted was a boyfriend, someone to hang out with, maybe fall in love with. Maybe even marry and have a family with someday. Dave's a great guy. We were so good together. Why would he ask me to make a choice like that?*

The thing was, there was no choice. Not when he put it as bluntly as that. He hadn't even said, "You have to choose between me and your church" or "between me and your religion."

He had said, "You have to choose between me and your God." Danielle loved Dave. He was there, warm and real and present, and God was far away in the distant night sky. Yet God was closer than her own skin, real and inside her too. She couldn't choose anyone over God. Not when you put it like that.

Ten years later Danielle looks back and likes the decision she made. She's married now to a guy who shares her faith. Together they're raising two children to love Jesus; together they're helping out in their church. She's glad she waited for God's timing, God's "Mr. Right" instead of her own.

But hearing her story, I can't help wondering . . . What if Dave hadn't stated that choice so bluntly? Because the fact is, a lot of people in our lives ask us to make that choice. But very few are as direct as Dave. Very few will say, "It's God or me. Make a choice."

Most of us could probably take a stand for God if it were put that simply. It usually isn't. Usually we're asked to make a series of small choices—little compromises, in which we undermine our standards or neglect our time with God or stay silent when someone demeans the values we care about. Little choices, piled one on top of another—tiny opportunities to say yes or no to God. Boyfriends, girlfriends, just friends—all may ask us to choose between them and God without ever putting the choice into words.

I know I used to waste a lot of time when I was younger, wondering if I'd hold up under persecution. If I were a Christian in some developing country dictatorship where Christianity is outlawed, what would I say when the military police came to break up my house church meeting? Would I stand true for my faith? What if I were Cassie Bernall at Columbine High, facing a gunman with the question "Do you believe in God?" Could I say yes?

Maybe I could. But does that matter if I say no to God over and over, in a thousand different ways? If I stand by silently when someone belittles His name? If I refuse to imitate His example of love when I deal with someone I dislike? If I let down His standard when I'm at a party with friends?

Very few of us are lucky enough to get those big decision moments when we realize how clear our choice really is. Danielle got one of those moments. She rose to the occasion and chose God. Maybe today I'll have to choose between God and someone else, something else, that's important to me. And if the choice is not spelled out in clear black letters on a white background, if it's subtle or small or easy to miss, I hope I'll see it. I hope I'll see it and make Danielle's choice.

Choose for yourselves this day whom you will serve. . . . But as for me and my household, we will serve the Lord. Joshua 24:15, NIV.

THINK IT THROUGH

1. When was the last time you were faced with the choice of putting someone or something before God? How did you respond?

2. Is it easier for you to stand for God in the "big choices" or in the "little choices"?

3. Is there someone or something in your life that's consistently coming between you and God? Are you ready to give that up to Him?

43.

HARD TO SAY "I'M SORRY"

Two words weren't used much in Lynda's home as she was growing up: "I'm sorry."

I guess there are only two reasons not to say I'm sorry—either
because you never do anything wrong, or because you refuse to admit
you did anything wrong. Very few of us fall into the first category.

About 30 years ago a novel and movie called *Love Story* popu-
larized the slogan "Love means never having to say you're sorry."
The theory, I suppose, was that if you truly loved someone, you
would never do anything to hurt them, so you would never have to
apologize for anything. If I remember the plot of *Love Story* correctly, the girl dies of cancer before she and her young husband have
a chance to raise kids, pay down a mortgage, or do most of the other
things that lead people into "I'm sorry" situations. Perhaps if you can
keep your love story short and sweet enough, you can live by the
never-say-I'm-sorry rule.

But let's face it, for most of us love means saying a lot of "I'm
sorry." It means being sensitive enough to recognize when an
apology is needed and being big enough to take the blame and ask
for forgiveness.

On the other hand, being arrogant, smug, and self-satisfied really
does mean never having to say you're sorry. Maybe Lynda's family
fell a little more into that category. Even when her parents were obviously wrong they never apologized for anything. It was the kind

of house where "Father knows best," and so does Mother, and they never paused to question whether they might, on occasion, have made a mistake.

Growing up in that home wasn't easy for Lynda, but she survived, and moved out, and met her husband-to-be, and started living out her own *Love Story*. And everything went well, until they day Lynda and Ben had their first big argument.

It was one of those arguments in which both were to blame. Ben did something thoughtless—scheduled a meeting at work on the evening of Lynda's birthday, when they had planned to go out to dinner. He could have easily scheduled it at a different time, but once it was set and everyone was notified, it couldn't be changed, and Lynda's birthday dinner had to be shifted.

That part was clearly Ben's fault—but then, in the argument that followed, Lynda said a number of hurtful things, such as "You don't care about anyone but yourself!" and "Why are you so stupid?" and other comments of that type. Everyone's feelings got hurt, and they both retreated to separate corners of their tiny apartment to lick their wounds.

Lynda, crying alone in the bedroom, didn't know where to go from there. She and Ben had never had a serious fight during their whirlwind romance. Her childhood memories of her parents' arguments had involved days of giving each other the cold shoulder and silent treatment until gradually things returned to "normal"—the fight was never supposed to be mentioned again, but it seemed to linger under the surface like a badly healed scar until the next fight erupted. She couldn't stand to think of living like that with Ben. Already her anger and hurt pride were being overcome by the desire to make things right—but she had no idea where to begin.

Then there was a tap at the bedroom door. "Can I come in, Lynda?" Ben asked.

"I guess so," Lynda sniffed.

He came in and sat on the foot of the bed. "I just wanted to say, honey, that I'm really sorry I forgot your birthday and scheduled that meeting. It was thoughtless of me. I can't change it now, but I'll try to make it up to you with a wonderful evening out the next night. Can you forgive me?"

Lynda was speechless. She had literally never heard someone close to her make a speech like that. She thought people talked that way only in movies and novels.

"I—uh—yes—I mean, yes, it's OK, I—don't worry about it." The words "I forgive you" sounded too formal and official. Ben reached out and took her hand, and she hugged him. Everything was OK again.

Except that Lynda realized she should apologize too, for the things she'd said. It was her turn to say "I'm sorry," but she just couldn't.

The next time they had an argument, a few months down the road, it was clearly Lynda's fault. Instead of the hurt feelings lasting a half hour, they lasted nearly a day as Lynda struggled with her reluctance to say "I'm sorry." Finally she turned to Ben at bedtime and said, "Um, I'm sorry—about what happened. I didn't mean it." It wasn't much next to his humble, well-crafted apology, but Ben accepted it.

Throughout the early years of their marriage the same pattern continued. Whenever they had a disagreement (which, fortunately, didn't happen too often), Ben would quickly and humbly apologize and ask for Lynda's forgiveness. When it was Lynda's turn, she would struggle with over the words "I'm sorry." They seemed so difficult to say.

Gradually Lynda came to understand that saying "I'm sorry" was hard for her because it hadn't been part of the vocabulary in her family's home. It felt as if she was learning a foreign language. But under Ben's loving tutelage she began to learn.

Lynda and Ben had a baby, who grew into a toddler. One day in a crowded supermarket little Jillian dawdled in the aisle, playing with a toy she had brought, while Lynda charged ahead trying to get her shopping done. Jillian wasn't disobeying, just being a normal 3-year-old—but Lynda was stressed out, and she lost her temper, as parents have done since the dawn of time. She yelled at Jillian, picked her up roughly, and sat her in the shopping cart. And Jillian, naturally, began to cry.

Lynda felt terrible. She pulled out a Kleenex to dry Jillian's tears and wrapped her daughter in a big hug. "It's all right, Jillian. Mommy shouldn't have yelled at you like that. That was wrong of me. I'm sorry." And though her 3-year-old couldn't really understand the concept of forgiveness, Lynda added, "Please forgive me."

As she felt Jillian's arms tighten around her, Lynda realized she'd said the words her own mother and father had never said. *That was wrong of me. I'm sorry.* With a quick prayer of thanks to God—and to Ben—she was at last becoming fluent in her second language, the language of love.

> **Be kind to one another, tenderhearted,**
> **forgiving one another, even as God**
> **in Christ forgave you. Ephesians 4:32, NKJV.**

THINK IT THROUGH

1. Are there parts of the "language of love" that are foreign to you because they were never used in your home? Have you begun learning new ways to communicate with those you love?

2. If you're married or in a serious relationship, do you think God has used you to teach your partner any lessons about love—or vice versa? What do you think God's plan is for single people to learn love's lessons?

44.

MATCHING DREAMS

Why, we're so much alike—one night even our dreams matched," laughed George.

Abby nodded her head. "That's right, we even had matching dreams," she agreed. She placed her wrinkled hand over George's. "The other night I dreamed our old washing machine finally gave out. I couldn't wash anything—laundry was pilin' up all around the place."

"And that very same night," George chimed in, "I dreamed I was pawin' through my drawer, lookin' for socks, and I couldn't find one clean sock. Not one!"

"So when we woke up in the morning and told each other our dreams, George just said, 'Well, I guess that explains it! Your washin' machine broke down, so my sock drawer was empty.'" Abby smiled, remembering. "We sure had a good laugh over that."

Julie sat at George and Abby's kitchen table, tracing patterns on the tablecloth with her fingertip, smiling at the obvious joy the old couple shared. George and Abby were like adopted grandparents to Julie's family. She'd been coming to visit them as long as she could remember. When she was younger she'd sometimes get a little bored with their stories and reminiscences, but now that she was engaged to be married herself, she found herself watching the older couple closely, trying to understand what made them so special.

It wasn't anything complicated—it was just that George and

Matching Dreams

Abby loved each other so much. Julie's own parents were divorced, and while she knew plenty of other married couples, she had never seen any couple who seemed to fit together as perfectly as George and Abby.

They got a lot of enjoyment out of the story of their matching dreams, but they also had matching dreams in a deeper sense. It seemed as if they'd always shared the same goals, the same hopes, the same vision. They both loved God and were committed to serving Him. They both cared about reaching out to people and made their home a warm and welcoming place.

But it was the way they treated each other that caught Julie's attention most. She knew plenty of married people who called each other "love" or "honey" or "darling" the way George and Abby did, but George's and Abby's love for each other went far beyond the surface, far beyond words. They treated each other with respect. There were never any put-downs, not even the teasing kind. Even their jokes were always kind, always intended to build each other up rather than to tear down.

That's what I want, Julie decided. If she and Steve could have that kind of marriage, that kind of mutual respect and oneness—that would be a dream worth working toward.

Julie got married a few months later and moved away. Not long after, her mom mentioned on the phone that Abby wasn't doing too well. "Mostly just old age, I guess," Julie's mom said, "and all the problems that go along with it. After all, she is 87. She's in the hospital, but I don't know how much they can do for her."

A few weeks later the inevitable call came. "Julie, honey, I know you'll be sorry to hear this," her mom said, "but Abby passed away last night. In her sleep. It was very peaceful."

"Oh, how sad," Julie responded. "Poor George. I wonder what he'll do without her."

Everyone thought just as Julie did—that George wouldn't last long after Abby's death. They had been so completely united—so dependent on each other—it was impossible to imagine one without the other. "I give him a few months, that's all," one friend said. "He'll just fade away without Abby."

But George surprised them all. Yes, he grieved for Abby. Yes, he was lonely without her. "But that's when I realized," Julie says, "that there was something in George's life even greater than his love and devotion to Abby—and that was his love and devotion to the Lord." George was crushed by Abby's death, but not destroyed. His faith remained—a faith strong enough to believe that Abby's death was part of God's plan, and that he, George, still had a part to play in that plan, even with Abby gone.

"It was amazing to me," says Julie, "that his love for the Lord could be so great that it carried him after losing the most important person in his life."

Once Julie had wished that she and her new husband might have a love as close and enduring as George and Abby had had. She still wanted that. But she wanted something else more—a love for the Lord as strong and powerful as they had shared. That was the foundation that made it possible for them to carry on living and sharing the same dream—through life and beyond.

For this reason a man will leave his father and mother and be united to his wife, and they will become one flesh. Genesis 2:24, NIV.

THINK IT THROUGH

1. Is a relationship like George and Abby's possible only for Christians? If not, how can you explain the fact that those who don't know God can demonstrate true love for each other?

2. Would being this close to another human being involve sacrifice? What do you think you might have to give up to have a relationship this close? Would it be worth it?